KT-558-004

B.S.U.C. - LIBRARY

00288651

DISCARD

The Storm

The Storm

The World Economic Crisis
and What It Means

VINCE CABLE

Atlantic Books

LONDON

Published in Great Britain in 2009 by Atlantic Books,
an imprint of Grove Atlantic Ltd.

Copyright © Vincent Cable, 2009

The moral right of Vincent Cable to be identified as the author of
this work has been asserted by her in accordance with the Copyright,
Designs and Patents Acts of 1988.

All rights reserved. No part of this publication may be reproduced,
stored in a retrieval system, or transmitted in any form or by any
means, electronic, mechanical, photocopying, recording, or otherwise,
without the prior permission of both the copyright owner and the
above publisher of this book.

Every effort has been made to trace or contact all copyright holders.
The publishers will be pleased to make good any omissions or rectify
any mistakes brought to their attention at the earliest opportunity.

2 3 4 5 6 7 8 9

A CIP catalogue record for this book is available from the British Library.

ISBN: 978 184887 057 4

Printed in Great Britain by CPI Mackays, Chatham ME5 8TD

Atlantic Books
An imprint of Grove Atlantic Ltd
Ormond House
26–27 Boswell Street
London
WC1N 3JZ

www.atlantic-books.co.uk

BATH SPA UNIVERSITY
NEWTON PARK LIBRARY
Class No.
338.9 CAB
Donation 12/5/09

Contents

Introduction

For the best part of sixty years the world has enjoyed a remarkable period of apparently ever expanding production, rising living standards and integration across frontiers. The clichés surrounding globalization are tediously predictable. The End of History. The End of Geography. Booming trade and foreign investment. A technological revolution resulting in cross-border communications of unprecedented speed. Financial markets able to transmit vast sums of money across national frontiers at the click of a switch. Industrial growth reaching new records. Mass tourism and migration. Rapidly emerging markets.

In the wake of the international banking crisis and the advancing recession, the inexorable suddenly looks uncertain. Hubris is giving way to nemesis. Panic and the collapse of apparently secure financial institutions have reawakened long-dormant fears about the stability and sustainability of what seemed to be unstoppable, foolproof, historical forces of economic expansion. History teaches us, moreover, that individual and collective stupidity, greed and complacency act as powerful countervailing forces to what seems like unstoppable progress.

The late nineteenth century offered – at least for those parts of the world experiencing economic and technological take-off – a comparable period of growth and successful 'globalization'. And then, things went horribly wrong. War, inflation, financial collapse, deflation, protectionism and another global war. Two generations later, we reassure ourselves that lessons have been learned, that the same mistakes will not be repeated, and that peaceful international economic integration will not again be destroyed by government incompetence and atavistic nationalism. We hope.

That hope has rested on confidence that the past has been remembered and properly understood. Yet there is, in the present febrile atmosphere of financial and wider economic crisis, in other countries as well as our own, a collective amnesia, a preoccupation with the immediate future and frantic efforts to stave off the next disaster. So far at least, governments have shown a proper sense of urgency and a recognition that if they do not hang together they will hang separately. But there are influential voices, as in the 1930s, urging a retreat behind protective barricades and disowning the liberal economic system, which is the only one that we know actually works.

The three disastrous decades from 1914 to 1945 have provided, for succeeding generations of policy makers, a set of lessons on what to avoid. These lessons were embedded in the process of post-war reconstruction under the political leadership of the USA and the intellectual leadership of Maynard Keynes and his disciples. Pre-eminent among them is a set of rules and institutions to prevent conflict, economic as well as political. The GATT (later the WTO), the Bretton Woods institutions and, in Europe, the Common Market, all had the objective of preventing a destructive cycle of 'beggar my neighbour' economics, and a commitment to liberalizing trade and capital flows within a set of agreed rules. The emergence later of new collective problems, such as global environmental threats, has reinforced this sense of cooperation as a public good.

A second and related aim was to ensure that, unlike pre-war Japan and Germany, emerging economic powers could achieve their aspirations for development through assimilation into democratic and market-based economic arrangements. The EU has been successful in relation to southern and then eastern Europe, and the United States has taken the lead in embracing the newly industrializing countries of east and south-east Asia as well as Latin America. But the European Union is struggling with the bigger challenges of Turkey and the former Soviet Union. Russia is retreating from the limited degree of integration achieved through the G8. India played a leading role in the collapse of the WTO negotiations. And the rapid emergence and only partial acceptance of China as an economic and political superpower lie at the heart of current global financial instability.

A further set of lessons arising from the post-war settlement related to the respective roles of the state and the market in successful modern economies.

There has, of course, been vigorous debate about the size and scope of the public sector. But it has been a central tenet of post-war economic policy, at least in the West and increasingly in emerging-market economies, that it is the job of government to facilitate the workings of open, capitalist economies: countering cycles of inflation and unemployment through macroeconomic management; providing safety nets through welfare states of varying generosity; and regulating markets where there are egregious failures.

In the last two decades the pendulum swung, particularly in the Anglo-Saxon world, towards deregulation. This appeared to have borne fruit in accelerating growth and widening opportunities for hundreds of millions of people in the rich and poor worlds. Yet the proclamation in the 1990s of 'the end of history', though rightly acknowledging the triumph of liberal systems, was hubristic and premature. It prejudged that governments would avoid or, at the very least, deal successfully with challenges such as the present combination of a systemic crisis in the financial system, price shocks, cyclical downturn and painful structural adjustment: The Storm. If the crisis is not managed well, we can expect to see some fundamental challenges to the whole post-war order.

The main focus of attention has been on a financial crisis centring on the banking system, the worst in scale and scope since the inter-war period. But there have been other, inter-acting forces of instability. One of the currents feeding the storm has been a severe price shock: a sharp increase – now partially reversed, at least for the moment – in the prices of energy, raw materials and food. Much of the recent commentary has been cast in apocalyptic terms. The End of Oil. Malthusian Famine. Or, more generally, a reassertion of the 'Limits to Growth' thinking that flowered briefly in the 1970s. The collapse in commodity prices of late 2008 has made these hyperbolic assertions look very dated, even ridiculous; but we are reminded nonetheless of the high level of instability in markets for commodities as well as financial products.

Arguably, the latest shock is the sixth since the Napoleonic Wars, when a period of economic expansion and disrupted trade and production sent the prices of food and industrial raw materials through the roof. There were similar episodes in the 1850s, coinciding with the Crimean War; at the turn of the nineteenth century; and in the early 1970s, when we experienced the first oil shock. Each of these episodes was, of course, unique, complex and painful in different ways. But we now know from experience what happens when world economic growth outstrips natural resource capacity. Prices explode and then subside as a new balance is established. Experience shows that governments can take sensible steps to mitigate the impact of commodity price shocks, but these do not include a retreat into autarky, even the mild Gallic version that manifests itself as farm protection. There is a risk that recent talk of 'food security' or 'energy security' presages precisely such a retreat, especially if insecurity is reinforced by fears of deepening recession.

The commodity price shock coincided in Britain, the USA, Spain and elsewhere with the creation, and now the bursting, of a bubble in the housing market. Indeed, the two things are probably linked through the same process of monetary expansion and contraction. But in addition, a new generation of home buyers, property investors and builders had persuaded itself that prices only ever go up, and that property was a guaranteed way to accumulate wealth. All historical experience should have taught us otherwise. There were regular building cycles in the UK throughout the eighteenth century, which were measured by historians as having an average of sixteen years from peak to peak, with continuing boom and bust cycles in the nineteenth century.

There is room for debate about the precise speed of the metronome, but a contemporary analyst, Fred Harrison, looking at the twentieth century has come up with a figure of nineteen years. And throughout modern economic history, the bursting of property bubbles has been one of the key trigger factors leading to earlier periods of recession: Britain in the 1990s; Japan at the same time and for longer; and now the USA. By now, governments should have worked out how to recognize and anticipate these bubbles, and, at least, deal with them in a rational manner. Yet the British and American governments are treating the problem as if it were being encountered for the first time.

The bursting of the house price bubble has been linked in turn to the so-called 'credit crunch', around which much of this book centres. Bank credit has been drastically curtailed in the wake of a collapse of confidence in the financial system. Markets have become fearful of contamination by bad debt, originating in US sub-prime mortgages, but now more widely diffused. The idea that financial markets are prone to excess, instability and panic is hardly new. The experience has been endlessly repeated throughout history. If we go back to John Stuart Mill, his analysis of irrational market expectations, based on a dramatic financial crisis in 1824–6 (and earlier events in 1712, 1784, 1793, 1810–11, 1814–15 and 1819), describes very precisely what happens when a 'frenzy' of 'over-trading' leads to a cycle of intense speculation, crisis and depression: 'the failure of a few great commercial houses occasions the ruin of many of their numerous creditors. A general alarm ensues and an entire stop is put for the time being to all dealings upon credit: many persons are thus deprived of their usual accommodation and are unable to continue their business.'

Today, illiquid small businesses, and people trying unsuccessfully to remortgage their houses, will know exactly what Mill meant by the loss of 'the usual accommodation' by their once-friendly local bank managers. That earlier crisis was eventually stopped by borrowing money from France and by distributing a stash of old banknotes found to have been hidden away in the Bank of England. Today's crisis is very much more complicated, but has the same basic architecture.

The history of financial bubbles should now be well understood. However, successive generations of financiers and investors have deluded themselves that they have, at last, found a foolproof way to manufacture riches without undue exertion: tulips in the seventeenth century; South Sea stocks in the eighteenth; various manias over emerging markets in the nineteenth; through to Wall Street in the 1920s. Then, more recently, there has been Latin American sovereign debt in the 1970s, Japanese land in the 1980s, British and Scandinavian housing in the 1980s (again), the Asian Tigers in the mid-1990s, new communications technology in the late 1990s, as well as our latest excitements. A generation ago, Hyman Minsky described the mechanisms by which financial markets regularly overreach themselves, through excessive leverage, excessive risk-taking, greed and folly, leading to panic and then to 'revulsion': the stopping of credit. He would have recognized the contemporary commentators, bankers and politicians who, as with each preceding generation, have solemnly asserted that the world has changed and financial crises have become less likely, thanks to new technology and their own collective cleverness. Of course, they have not. And it is precisely the high level of technological sophistication and international economic integration that makes the recurrence of financial mania and crashes now so far-reaching and worrying.

I start with the past, since it reminds us that, whatever the contemporary uncertainties, there are lessons to be learned from what has gone before. This does not mean that I am a deterministic fatalist. Every stock exchange crash and banking crisis does not need to be followed by a Great Depression. Every burst property market bubble does not need to be followed by a Japanese decade of stagnation. Every boom in food prices does not mean that poor people should go hungry. There are better and worse ways of dealing with these problems, and hopefully historical perspective and comparative experience should help us to find the better ways.

It is especially important to reflect on the wider historical context, since the current combination of circumstances is particularly dangerous and potentially very destructive. The management of a collapsing housing market combined with a severe crisis of confidence in financial markets and institutions, as in the USA and the UK, would be difficult at the best of times. But, coincidentally, policy has been complicated by the need to respond to an inflationary commodity price shock, particularly in oil (and gas). And the commodity price shock originated with booming demand in emerging countries, led by China, whose economies are no longer dominated by the Western world and which are only tenuously integrated into the rules and institutions overseeing the world economy. Indeed, there is a plausible argument, discussed in detail in chapter 4, that China's emergence, and the imbalance in trade and in domestic savings and investment between the USA and China, explain the financial bubbles of this century. The unifying thread of common interest is being frayed to breaking point, as we have seen with the collapse of the world trade talks and the attempts being made to blame the current crisis on American self-indulgent weakness or manipulative Chinese Communist authorities.

Yet if there is one lesson above all to be learned from historical experience, it is that nothing is more beguiling or more destructive than the siren voices of nationalism and its contemporary variants. Inter-war fascism has disappeared, but there are more subtle voices seeking to scapegoat foreigners, especially yellow and brown ones, or migrant workers in our midst, or else setting out a protectionist programme in the name of food or job or energy security. Less potent, but also dangerous, are those who, under a red flag – and sometimes under a green flag – work to destroy the liberal economic order and suppress markets and capitalism altogether. A century and a half ago in *Das Kapital*, Karl Marx produced a remarkably prescient description of where we are now, which may inspire some to revisit his prescription:

> Owners of capital will stimulate the working class to buy more and more of expensive goods, houses and mechanical products, pushing them to take more and more expensive credits, until their debt becomes unbearable. The unpaid debt will lead to bankruptcy of banks, which will have to be nationalised, and the State will have to take the road which will eventually lead to communism.

This conjuncture of extreme events and an increasingly hostile political environment has been described as a 'perfect storm'. This short book tries to describe how that storm originated and where it might lead.

Economic storms, like those in nature, come and go. They cannot be abolished. But, as with hurricanes and typhoons, they can be anticipated and planned for and a well-coordinated emergency response, involving international cooperation, can mitigate the misery. They also test out the underlying seaworthiness of the vessels of state. The fleet has been plying a gentle swell for some years and making impressive progress. But big waves are already exposing some weaknesses. SS *Britannia*, said to be unsinkable, has sprung a leak, and the vast supertanker *USA* is listing badly. Passengers and crews are starting to panic and have noticed that most of the life rafts are reserved for those in First Class. How many ships will finally make it back to port in good order after the storm is in doubt.

1

Trouble on the Tyne

On 13 September 2007, exceptionally long queues started to form outside branches of the Northern Rock bank across Britain. They were not queuing to pay their bills or to talk to the bank manager about a new loan. They were frightened. They wanted to withdraw their savings. The Bank of England had announced that it was supporting the bank, which was in financial difficulties. Depositors, far from being reassured, were alarmed. And as the television broadcast pictures of worried savers queuing to take out their money, others joined them. On one day £1 billion was withdrawn. A few days later, the panic ended when the Chancellor of the Exchequer fully guaranteed all the bank's deposits. But Britain's financial establishment had been shaken to the core. Britain had experienced its first 'run' on a bank since Overend Gurney in 1866.

A country that prided itself on being in the forefront of financial innovation and sophistication had been shamed by the kind of disaster normally experienced in the most primitive banking systems. The only visual images most British people had of banking panics were television pictures of bewildered and angry Russian *babushkas* impoverished by pyramid-selling schemes disguised as banks in the chaotic aftermath of communism, or ancient black and white photographs of Mittel-Europeans desperately trying to force the doors of imposing but barricaded buildings in the 1920s. But this was Britain in the twenty-first century!

For those not caught up in the panic there was a collective national embarrassment, like that experienced when Heathrow Airport's Terminal 5 didn't work or when a national sports team is humiliated. But there was a deeper anxiety when it gradually emerged that those managing an economy built in substantial measure on success in financial services had no effective system for protecting bank deposits, no set of principles governing bank failure and no clear idea what the mantra of 'lender of last resort' actually meant. It was a little like discovering that one of the country's leading obstetricians didn't have the first idea how to effect the delivery of a large baby because all his experience had been with small ones.

———

The full saga of Northern Rock has been well described elsewhere and I do not need to repeat the story, even though I was involved in it as a politician. The reason why Northern Rock was important in the wider context was not merely that it exposed the inadequacy of regulation and regulators, but that it was the first major institutional victim of a global banking crisis and the credit crunch. (Arguably, BNP–Paribas was hit a few weeks earlier and had closed two of its funds, and HSBC had, with some prescience, warned of large losses on US sub-prime lending some six months before – but it was Northern Rock that brought home, very publicly, the existence of a serious banking problem.)

The Rock had once been a highly regarded, Newcastle-based building society, with a long-standing reputation for financial prudence and a strong commitment to its Tyneside community. Its origins lay in the tradition of Victorian self-help which produced friendly societies and other mutual institutions – owned collectively by those who deposited money with them – channelling savings into mortgage lending and other investments. The Conservative government legislated for the demutualization of building societies as part of a wider deregulation of financial markets, in the belief that access to shareholders and freedom from traditional restraints would permit the societies to expand more rapidly and to compete directly with banks. I was one of those who campaigned at the time to stop demutualization, on the grounds that the traditional mutual model offered something different, and more financially attractive to investors and borrowers, from the banks. A decade later demutualization was, effectively, stopped. But Northern Rock had already escaped the constraints of mutuality in 1997, following the Abbey National, the Halifax and others.

When it converted from a mutual to a commercial bank, it initially sought to maintain its community focus, and the new PLC was launched alongside a charitable foundation with a guaranteed share of the bank's profits. The foundation has subsequently done much valued work in the north of England. But the management team, led from 2001 by Mr Adam Applegarth, had bigger ambitions for the bank – and themselves – than remaining as a small to middle-ranking player in the banking industry, known to the public mainly for its sponsorship of Newcastle United. They hatched an ambitious plan to capture a lion's share of the UK mortgage market. There were two problems. The first was how to raise the money to lend, since building societies traditionally accumulated funding by the slow process of attracting deposits. The second was how to persuade house buyers to take mortgages from Northern Rock rather than their competitors. They hit upon an audacious business plan designed to solve both problems.

Funds were to be raised not from depositors but from mortgage-backed securities. There was an appetite in financial markets for packages of mortgages sold on by banks to other institutions through wholesale markets in the City of London. Banks have long augmented their resources by market borrowing (one reason why they have been able to expand faster than the more conservative, mutual building societies), and in the last decade there has been a rapid growth in this new, more sophisticated form of borrowing, known as 'securitization'. But Northern Rock took borrowing to extremes; it raised 75 per cent of its mortgage-lending funds from wholesale markets, whereas a more conservative bank such as Lloyds TSB raised only 25 per cent, with the rest coming from deposits. Northern Rock saw securitization as a way of rapidly expanding its market share. Then, to attract new business, Northern Rock pushed out the boundaries of what the industry regarded as prudent lending. The traditional mortgage loan, at most 90–95 per cent of the value of a property and up to three times the borrower's income, was already looking rather old-fashioned in the competitive but booming mortgage market around the turn of the century. Northern Rock was willing to go further than its competitors. There were 125 per cent 'Together' mortgages: that is, loans of 25 per cent more than the value of a house (in the form of a 95 per cent mortgage plus a 30 per cent top-up loan). In a world of ever increasing house prices, borrowers were assured that their property would soon be worth more than their debt. Loans were advanced on the basis of double the traditional three times income. The mortgages were sold with evangelical zeal, as part of a process of helping poor, working-class families to enjoy the freedom and inevitable capital gains of home ownership. Other banks followed suit in what was a very competitive market – precisely as the Conservative demutualizers had hoped.

The strategy worked, for a while. Share prices soared. Mr Applegarth acquired fast cars and a castle from his share of the profits. According to the *News of the World*, a mistress was rewarded with five mortgages and a property empire. In the marketplace, Northern Rock doubled its share of mortgage lending over three years; it held 20 per cent of the UK market (net of repayments) in the first half of 2007, giving it the largest share of new mortgages. It looked too good to be true – and it was. There was increasing critical comment in the financial press. Shrewd observers noticed that Mr Applegarth had quietly disposed of a large chunk of his personal shareholding. Shareholders picked up on the worrying reports, and the share price slid from a peak of £12 in February 2007 to around £8 in June after a profit warning, and then to £2 in the September 'run'. One crucially important body did not respond to these concerns: the financial regulator, the FSA, which to the end remained publicly supportive of Northern Rock's business model and did little to avert the coming disaster. Indeed, in July 2007 it even authorized a special dividend from the bank's capital.

In September the model collapsed, in the wake of the decline of the sub-prime lending market in the USA. Northern Rock was the closest UK imitator of the US sub-prime lenders whose 'ninja' loans – to those with no income, no job and no assets – were the source of rumours of defaults. Since so much sub-prime lending had been securitized, there was a wider collapse of confidence in mortgage-backed assets, which, it emerged, were often 'contaminated' by bad debts which were difficult to trace. The market dried up and Northern Rock was no longer able to raise funds to support its operations.

The process by which the Rock was then rescued and, six months later, nationalized, is a tangled and complex story. There were, however, amid the detail, two important issues of principle. The first was the need to strike the right balance between the perceived risk of creating a damaging shock to the whole banking system, if one bank were allowed to go bust, and the danger of moral hazard, if foolish and dangerous behaviour were to be rewarded by a bail-out. I shall pursue the wider ramifications of this issue in the next chapter. Suffice it to say that, having initially emphasized the latter concern, moral hazard, the Governor of the Bank of England was then prevailed upon to undertake a rescue.

The second issue was how to strike the right balance between public-sector and private-sector risk and reward as a result of the rescue operation. After protracted and expensive delays in order to try to secure a 'private-sector solution' – which, in the eyes of critics, including the author, would have 'nationalized risk and privatized profit' – the government nationalized the company, effectively expropriating the shareholders.

Although it was only a relatively small regional bank, Northern

Rock forms a central part of my story because it was the small hinge on which the British economy swung. It opened the door to the credit crunch and influenced the wider international financial markets. And its extreme mortgage-lending practices marked the outer limit of the home-lending boom, which is now bursting.

———

To describe the last decade of UK house price inflation as a 'bubble' does not do justice to it. Even in a notoriously volatile market there are few precedents in recorded British history, or in that of any other major country, for the scale of the inflation. There were booms in the late 1940s in the immediate aftermath of the Second World War (followed by two decades of depressed prices in the economic boom years when Britain had Never Had It So Good). There was a short, sharp spike in prices in 1971–3, followed by another slump until the mid-1980s, and then the boom of the late 1980s and early 1990s, which led to the painfully remembered era of home repossession and 'negative equity'. Measured in relation to average after-tax income, housing had proved – contrary to popular myth – a disappointing store of value. Looking at underlying trends, and ignoring boom and bust cycles over the post-war period, shares have beaten property – and so has working for a living. But from the nadir of 1995 to the zenith of 2007 house prices doubled from four and a half times earnings to more than nine times earnings. They more than doubled, increasing by 130 per cent in real terms (that is, relative to inflation). The increase was more extreme than in the USA or in any other major Western economy. It was more like a large balloon than a bubble, and as vulnerable to being burst.

Why did the balloon grow so big? Ms Kate Barker reported to the government that the explosion of prices was explained by a mixture of demographics and parochial NIMBYs using the planning system to obstruct new development. The only solution was to build more homes. A target of 223,000 new homes a year was set for the period 2001–16, and councils were instructed to find room for them, whether or not they liked the idea of concreting over back gardens and diminishing amounts of green space. Yet there was something not quite right about this explanation. The UK population has increased fairly steadily, from 50 million in the 1951 census to 60 million today, under much the same planning regime and without, until recently, triggering any sustained shift in the trend growth in house prices. One new factor since the mid-1990s has been net immigration – but a significant part of this (from eastern Europe) is related to the economic cycle and is temporary and reversible.

The panic about the housing 'shortage' had started earlier in the decade, when there was a fall in the annual construction rate from around 200,000 new homes per annum down to 142,000 in 2001–2. This was at a time when the government was predicting an annual increase in households of 223,000 in England and Wales. Ergo, prices must inevitably rise. But as the market saw unprecedented inflation in response to the 'shortage', the reality on the ground was different. Production – which had in any event fallen mainly because of a drop in public-sector, not owner-occupied, housing – recovered to 173,000 in 2006–7. And between 2001 and 2006, the number of households increased by only 80,000 a year, according to the Office for National Statistics. The more expensive houses became, the more children remained with mum and dad, the less family rows led to couples breaking up, and the more grannies were accommodated at home rather than separately in a big old house or a sheltered flat. There was something not quite right with the popular explanation that soaring prices were caused by too many households chasing too few houses.

There are other factors that explained the bubble rather better. Easy credit was the key. Competition among mortgage lenders produced a bewildering variety of mortgage products – 15,600 in July 2007. They were often aggressively marketed, on terms – in relation to income and property value – that enabled more and more people to enter the market. Northern Rock was not the only bank willing to lend 100 per cent or more of the value of a property and five or six times the borrower's income. The research firm Data Monitor suggests that 7 per cent of recent mortgages were made to people with a poor credit history, and another 5–6 per cent have been 'self-certified', requiring no proof of income.

As prices rose, the sense that property is a good investment – even an alternative to a pension – also grew. The growth of the buy-to-let market and of the market in second homes was in part due to speculation that prices would continue to rise, generating nominal wealth and the potential for capital gains. Ten per cent of mortgages are currently held by buy-to-let landlords, as against 1 per cent a decade ago. Another former mutual, Bradford & Bingley, specialized in this area of business. There are also an estimated 276,000 second homes, many of them unoccupied for much of the year (with another 200,000 second homes overseas), partly acquired for investment purposes. An academic study by David Miles explained 62 per cent of the doubling of prices over the course of a decade as being due to the expectation of future price rises, with rising population accounting for only 9 per cent of the price rise (increases in incomes and low real interest rates explain the rest). An IMF study of changes in house prices between 1997 and 2007 concluded that in the UK (as also in Ireland and the Netherlands) around 30 per cent of the increase in prices could not be explained by 'fundamentals', such as population, rising income and lower interest rates – compared with a figure of around 20 per cent for France, Australia and Spain, and only 10 per cent for the USA. Any market that is inflated by expectations of future price rises, supported by the easy availability of credit, has the character of a bubble. Bubbles burst. This one has done, with spectacular and worrying consequences.

What made the British housing price bubble so dangerous in economic terms was that it was so highly leveraged (that is, supported by debt). The thousands of first-time buyers who acquired what came to be known as 'suicide mortgages' of 125 per cent of the property value were merely the vanguard of an army marching to the rhythm of ever increasing house prices. They borrowed to the limits of their capacity, or beyond, in order to get a foothold on the housing ladder. Mainly because of mortgages, but partly also because of personal borrowing, average household debt has risen to 160 per cent of income, double the 1997 level – the highest of any developed country, and the highest in British economic history.

It might reasonably be asked why these developments were allowed to continue unchecked, not least by the guardians of financial stability in the Bank of England and by the political overlord of the economy, the Chancellor of the Exchequer. There were many expressions of anxiety about increasing personal debt, and it was clear that growing numbers of people were being encouraged – in some cases through aggressive promotion – to take on more debt than they could sensibly manage. In 2002, in the *Daily Express*, I published a warning about rising household debt and proposed a plan to address it. Then, in November 2003, I raised the issue with Gordon Brown in parliament, in the context of the Budget Report, only to be met with a contemptuous dismissal of the problem:

Dr Vincent Cable (Twickenham): Is not the brutal truth that with investment, exports and manufacturing output stagnating or falling, the growth of the British economy is sustained by consumer spending pinned against record levels of personal debt, which is secured, if at all, against house prices that the Bank of England describes as well above equilibrium level?

Mr Brown: The Hon. Gentleman has been writing articles in the newspapers, as reflected in his contribution, that spread alarm, without substance, about the state of the British economy ...

A more heavyweight intervention than mine was the warning of the Governor of the Bank of England, who was especially concerned about escalating housing prices. Although prices continued to increase for three more years, he failed, unaccountably, to return to the subject. He was presumably persuaded that house prices (as opposed to inflation in goods and services) were not his primary concern, or that the problem, if it existed, was manageable.

Those who were comfortable with the boom in house prices and debt argued that high levels of debt acquired through mortgages didn't really matter, because, unlike in the crash of the early 1990s, there were low interest rates and low unemployment. But there are some simple fallacies in that argument which are now being uncovered in the reality of burgeoning orders for house repossessions and growing numbers of households in arrears.

First, bank lending rates were indeed at a relatively low 7.5 per cent even at their peak in July 2007, as against 15 per cent at the end of the boom in the late 1980s. But inflation was much lower too (2.5 per cent versus 10 per cent), so the real cost of borrowing was much the same.

Second, the massive increase in house prices – and the willingness of the banks to lend – meant that the absolute size of mortgage debt, and therefore debt servicing, grew substantially. The average size of a mortgage increased from £40,000 in 1999 to around £160,000 before the market crashed. The cost of servicing the debt therefore became even more onerous than in the earlier periods of financial stress, despite lower interest rates. Debt servicing as a share of household income reached 20 per cent a year ago, higher than in the earlier peak year of 1991.

Third, even before unemployment rose alarmingly at the end of 2008, unemployment was not the only cause of breakdown in families' ability to service debt – so were illness, pregnancy, short-time working, small variations in incomes, and redundancy due to the constant churning of the labour market. Nor is there much by way of a safety net. After 1995 benefits no longer covered mortgage payments for the first nine months out of work, after which time it is usually too late (though the government has recently relaxed the conditions). Some households have tried to insure against temporary loss of income; but only one fifth have done so, and the policies have been so expensive and so hedged around with exclusions that the competition authorities have been moved to investigate the sharp practices involved.

The leverage of mortgage debt adds two new potent ingredients to the cocktail of problems created by a collapsing housing market. One is negative equity. If prices were to fall by 30 per cent from the peak – and that is now a very conservative assumption – an estimated 3–3.5 million households would be at risk of having housing debts greater than the value of their property. At the time of writing, indications were that the fall would be much bigger than 30 per cent. While negative equity is not a disaster for those people happy to stay put, it necessarily reduces families' wealth and their willingness to borrow further and spend. The other consequence of unsustainable debt service is mortgage arrears leading to repossession. It has been cheerfully assumed that there could not be a repetition of the early 1990s, when 300,000 people lost their homes in the space of five years. We are, however, unfortunately now heading in that direction, if not beyond it. Annual repossession rates are estimated at 45,000 in 2008, up from 27,000 in 2007, but are expected to rise, perhaps, to 75,000 in 2009.

The growth of second-charge mortgages on personal loans and the securitization of mortgages have meant that there has been a weakening in banking based upon personal relationships with bank managers; a default in payments now often automatically triggers a court reference, the first step on the road to repossession. For most, repossession means the loss of a home, and creates more pressure on the dwindling stock of social housing. There the new homeless are competing with the 80,000 already in temporary accommodation and the 1.7 million homeless (in England alone) on council lists waiting for social housing, usually because of overcrowding or unsatisfactory conditions in the private rented sector.

When housing bubbles have burst before, prices have fallen, restoring affordability and a new balance. This time things are not so straightforward. The bursting of the housing bubble coincides with, and is partially attributable to, the credit crunch: the unwillingness of banks to lend. Because the market in mortgage securities has collapsed, banks are no longer able to raise money, other than through new deposits, so their ability to make new loans has been sharply, brutally cut. As banks have adjusted – not before time – to more realistic levels of risk, they are demanding bigger deposits, of as much as 25 per cent of the value of a home, and often will not lend at all. First-time buyers, at the time of writing, were having to raise 100 per cent of their annual take-home pay in order to cover the up-front costs of buying a house. We have a perverse situation where prices have been falling but affordability has also been declining. Not surprisingly, demand has evaporated, driving the market down even further.

Thus what has happened is not a correction in the housing market, with a welcome fall in prices caused by increases in supply relative to demand. Instead, prices have fallen because of the cost of and non-availability of credit. And supply has fallen because of a collapse in confidence in the building industry. There is a danger that, if credit were once again to become easily available, there would then be a (temporary) reinflation of the bubble, creating the potential for another crash.

The problems of a deflating housing bubble do not end with householders in arrears or in negative equity. The bottom has fallen out of the market for new housing. New housing developments, for sale or for buy-to-let, have been coming to completion for which there are no buyers or tenants. Many buy-to-let landlords have fallen into arrears. And, behind them, developers have been left with unsaleable stock. There has been a dramatic impact on the house-building industry, with a decline in the number of houses built from 170,000 down to an estimated 100,000 in 2008, with the loss of 100,000 construction jobs, including specialist craft and professional skills which will be difficult to reassemble. House builders have seen their share prices fall dramatically and some have gone under. And because Britain's planning system links new social housing to new private housing, the supply of social housing has been dragged down too.

Then the emergence of bad debt among home buyers in a falling market has had knock-on effects on the banks that have lent the money. Banks with a large mortgage portfolio, like Northern Rock, Bradford & Bingley and Alliance & Leicester, have had to acknowledge the risk of large and growing losses on their mortgage books, added to the losses from other market activities. In the first half of 2008 profits were 50 per cent down on the same period last year, with the Royal Bank of Scotland/NatWest reporting heavy losses (as did the Alliance & Leicester before it was absorbed by Santander). Several of the big banks had to raise capital from investors, having been hit by losses and write-downs on their British mortgage business (and wider losses from the recession). All of this made banks respond in time-honoured fashion: by cracking down hard on those to whom they had been only too keen to lend in happier times. Then, in September, the generalized collapse of confidence in banks led to the virtual disappearance of the traditional specialist mortgage lenders. The share price of Bradford & Bingley collapsed and the bank was promptly nationalized in order to prevent a Northern Rock-style saga. Halifax–Bank of Scotland (HBOS) was absorbed by Lloyds in order to prevent its collapsing in turn, before both had to be saved and recapitalized by the government, as was the Royal Bank of Scotland/NatWest. By this stage we were no longer dealing with a British housing and banking problem but with a global financial crisis, and I return to that bigger story in the next chapter.

The combined effect of the credit crunch, the deteriorating housing market, and the squeeze on living standards from the earlier hike in energy and food prices created the conditions for a recession. At the end of 2008 recession psychology was taking over rapidly. Consumers had become very anxious. They were reluctant to spend. Retail sales were falling sharply. And this in turn led to a slowdown in production, workers were being laid off, more people were unable to sustain mortgage and other debt payments, and pessimism was deepening in a vicious circle. At some point producers or consumers or both will recover their nerve and start to spend and invest, but such a turning point is nowhere in sight. Even the government, which has no incentive to maximize gloom, has acknowledged that there will be a recession, perhaps a deep one, before a possible recovery in 2010. Deflation has already arrived in Britain with retail prices falling by 2.5 per cent in the last quarter of 2008. One of the central premises of post-war Keynesian economics has been that government policy measures should be used to stimulate demand during a recession. And the shared understanding from previous financial crises, notably that of the 1930s, has been that such intervention has to be decisive and rapid.

———

The obvious first step was to cut interest rates. It is common ground among both monetarists and Keynesians that this is the first and quickest way to stimulate demand. One problem has been that the government has transferred the power to set interest rates to the Bank of England, which has an explicit mandate to use interest rates to curb consumer price inflation, which at the height of the crisis was running well above the official target level of 2 per cent. The Bank of England was initially torn between its commitment to combat inflation and a wish to stimulate the economy with interest rate cuts. There was no easy answer to this dilemma. Faced with precisely the same problem, the eurozone authorities initially opted to raise rates and the USA to cut them, because they assessed the balance of risks in different ways. But by October 2008 it had become clear that the British banking system was caught up in a global financial crisis of massive and dangerous proportions. One of the few remedies open to the authorities in order to prevent a slump was a big cut in the interest rate. For those of us who believed in the principle of operational independence for the Bank of England there was a dilemma: to defer to the Bank, which seemed to be moving too slowly, or to call publicly for a deep cut, recognizing exceptional circumstances. I called for a rate cut of 2 per cent. The Bank of England got there in stages, helped by a concerted 0.5 per cent cut agreed between central banks in October 2008, followed by a unilateral cut of 1.5 per cent, to 3 per cent, in November, and a further cut to 2 per cent in December. These cuts will undoubtedly have an impact, but in the short run the normal transmission mechanism has largely broken down. The credit crunch is restricting the supply of credit, whatever the price. Monetary authorities in the UK and elsewhere have recognized that parallel action is necessary to restore normal bank lending, but also that further cuts may well be necessary, perhaps to zero, as well as unorthodox measures to boost the supply of money, as discussed in chapter 7.

There has been more controversy over whether it is also necessary to stimulate the economy by running a larger budget deficit. This is already happening automatically, since as the economy slows there will be weaker tax receipts from personal and corporate income, VAT and stamp duty. But there is anxiety that, even without the impact of recession, the government has been running an excessive, structural, deficit. The OECD, among others, was very critical of the British government's gradual drift into larger, unplanned deficits, even before the problem of the recession arose. In December 2008 there was an increasingly polarized debate about whether Britain's public finances were strong enough to permit a small fiscal stimulus, of around 1 per cent of GDP, on top of a deficit of 7 per cent of GDP, expected in any event. Critics argue that if the government's borrowing requirement spirals out of control, then the cost of borrowing in international markets will rise on the fear of sovereign default, perhaps in a dramatic way. A prolonged, steep fall in sterling against the dollar and the euro suggested a wider problem of confidence.

Because so much of the uncertainty and worry besetting the UK economy has centred on the housing market, there has been an argument to the effect that any attempt to rescue the economy from a downward spiral of declining confidence, declining spending, and declining activity should centre on shoring up house prices. The banks, as well as builders and property owners, are, unsurprisingly, proponents of this approach. Various ideas have been canvassed, including direct or indirect state guarantees for new loans, stamp duty suspension or reduction, or the state funding of mortgage arrears through the benefit system. A moderate reduction in stamp duty was attempted in September 2008 and sank without trace. There has also been a modest programme to assist people who are out of work to pay their mortgages. But the government and the Bank of England have essentially declined any suggestions that they should stop the housing market adjusting through a substantial fall in prices. This adjustment is now taking place and all the indicators are that the market will adjust brutally, and perhaps too far.

The most dramatic and far-reaching interventions in the UK economy have not been in monetary or fiscal policy, nor in the housing market, but on the banking system. In that respect Britain was caught up in a wider international banking crisis. But this is not to minimize the specific shock to the British economy of having several banks nationalized, others partly nationalized, and others still dependent for their survival on government guarantees. Britain also pioneered what became a collective response to the crisis in the form of recapitalizing banks through government capital.

The global nature of the crisis has left in its wake a somewhat confusing and unsatisfactory political debate, in which the government claims that the financial crisis and its aftermath of recession are problems whose origins lie exclusively overseas, while its critics, notably the Conservative opposition, simply blame the government for mismanagement. A balanced assessment has to be that there is both an international and a domestic dimension. Without diminishing in any way the global origins and nature of the crisis it is also necessary to debunk the self-serving myth that Britain has, in Gordon Brown's words, created an economic environment of 'no more boom and bust', and that the country is uniquely well placed to ride out the global storm. On the contrary, Britain's housing and debt bubbles have been larger than elsewhere; the government has relatively limited freedom of manoeuvre in fiscal policy because of structural deficits; and a large financial services sector, centred on the City of London, has exposed the UK to the full force of the gale that is blowing through international financial markets.

―――――――

These failings are not just technical, but reflect deep social currents. The extremity of Britain's housing bubble stems ultimately from a national obsession with property and property values. Those who feel that they must 'have a foot on the property ladder' are not just making a calculated assessment about the future value of a capital asset, but are buying into the notion that 'an Englishman's home is his castle' and into the concept of a 'property owning democracy'. Mrs Thatcher's brilliantly populist 'right to buy' policy – under which council tenants could buy their homes, usually at a hefty discount to the market price – contributed mightily to the idea of the 'first-time buyer' as an essential pillar of society, an iconic figure on a par with the self-sacrificing, saintly NHS nurse or the self-made entrepreneur. New Labour understood perfectly the importance of the icon: the sense of self-esteem and security that came from discovering that one's own bricks and mortar were worth more and more; the economic value and personal satisfaction derived from home and garden improvements. The plethora of TV property programmes and the domination of national newspapers by property supplements and house price stories reflected our national mania. It is not in the least surprising that a bubble in property prices was allowed to run out of control. The government now faces the uncontrolled fury of voters whose dreams of a property-based nirvana are now being cruelly dashed.

There was another set of British illusions that have played powerfully into the current crisis: the glamour of the City and the lure of Big Money. After the demise of much of Britain's manufacturing industry, the City emerged as a national success story. The banks and finance houses whose offices now define the skyline of London may be owned by foreigners, but they have chosen to operate here. Lots of Dick Whittingtons have discovered that the streets of London really are paved with gold. The City has sedulously cultivated an image of buccaneering, innovative entrepreneurship. Britain has been projected as a place with the cleverest, most hard-working and attractive financiers. A generation of brilliant young graduates with advanced numeracy has been persuaded, by lavish incentives, to devote their intelligence to financial inventiveness, rather than the more tedious and less lucrative alternatives of the laboratory or the classroom. There was a role, too, for the proles: smart young men with Estuary English, who could make a killing and accumulate previously unheard-of wealth on the dealing-floor.

All those bonuses may have financed the champagne and cocaine markets, but they percolated through too to the Treasury and the wider economy. Governments were seduced by this narrative, and politicians brought up on Trotsky and *The Ragged-Trousered Philanthropists* fought for the honour to be champions of the City.

There is now a brutal reappraisal taking place. Aspiring Dick Whittingtons are discovering that much of the gold was iron pyrites: 'fool's gold'. Brilliant financial innovators have been recognized as greedy or reckless or incompetent, or all three. Self-proclaimed, buccaneering entrepreneurs in the banking industry have been reduced to rattling a begging bowl and are dependent on the government bailing them out. Though the City remains an important industry, there are fewer illusions now that it has been seen to generate financial and wider economic instability, as well as wealth.

The impact of the simultaneous battering given to the ideal of owner-occupation and the reputation of financiers will only be fully understood with the passage of time, and much will depend on the severity of the storm. The challenge for the UK will be to manage a very painful correction and to achieve some rebalancing, between private- and public-sector housing, and between the regulation and deregulation of financial services.

What started as minor trouble on the Tyne has grown and turned into a major crisis for the UK economy. But the UK is merely one, modest, part of the global economy: barely 2 per cent of it. The collapse of confidence in financial markets and in what were, until recently, seen as stable institutions is a much wider phenomenon. To that bigger context, I now turn.

2

The Great Credit Contraction

For many Americans, hurricanes are a regular hazard. They happen frequently and are generally well prepared for. So it is with financial crises. In recent decades there have been episodes of extreme volatility in the prices of securities, property and commodities. There is usually a trail of damage, but it is temporary and superficial. But occasionally, as in nature, there is a financial super-storm of great destructive power. The biggest and most destructive within living memory (at least for the very old) was the Great Crash of 1929–32, which caused mass unemployment and a fall of one third in US GDP. It did not recover to 1929 levels for a decade. The experience shaped US policy, and politics, for a generation, perhaps two. Institutional memory of that event has been kept alive, not least by the Chairman of the Federal Reserve, Ben Bernanke, who studied it for his PhD thesis.

The question that has dominated those charged with responsibility for policy has been whether the tropical storm proceeding through the global banking system was developing into a full-blown hurricane, or merely a violent storm like the savings and loans crisis of the 1980s. The latter resulted in cumulative losses of $500 billion, but was contained, albeit at a substantial cost to the US taxpayer, without affecting the economy of the USA in a significant way, let alone that of the world. Another potentially destructive storm in 1999 centred on the collapse of the hedge fund Long Term Capital Management. Then there were, around the millennium, a bursting bubble in 'dot.com' shares in the USA and Europe, and financial crises in Asia – Thailand, South Korea, Malaysia and Taiwan – followed by a default on Russian debt. While these individual crises inflicted considerable damage on the countries concerned – a loss of over 30 per cent of GDP in Thailand, for example – there was no significant impact on the USA or the rest of the world economy.

It has become increasingly clear that the storm is not one of those lesser events, but one of the most destructive ever known: the equivalent of a Force 12 hurricane. The earlier storms blew over. The attitude of the US authorities, however, in each case, was that a major potential disaster could only be averted by applying the central lesson of the 1929–32 crash, which was the need to counter the deflationary effect of a financial crash by pursuing expansionary monetary policies. Faced, for example, with a potential systemic crash at the turn of the century, the authorities cut interest rates dramatically, from 6.5 per cent in 2000 to 1 per cent in 2003. It is a matter for conjecture whether dramatic intervention was necessary or desirable and whether it contributed to later, damaging, inflation in markets. But the apparent success of that strategy – albeit with three quarters of recession over the years 2000–1 – helped to elevate the then Chairman of the Federal Reserve, Alan Greenspan, to a status akin to beatification. It is just as well that beatification did not proceed to sainthood, since his freewheeling approach to financial regulation is now seen as a major cause of the more complex and deeper financial crisis that we are facing – perhaps a bigger crisis in scale and scope than has ever been seen before.

The immediate source of turbulence, and the trigger for the current global financial crisis, was the US mortgage market. As the economy recovered from the downturn of 2000–1 on the back of low interest rates, a veritable army of American Adam Applegarths pumped out enormous numbers of mortgages, often aimed at poorer families or those with a poor credit history. So-called 'ninja' loans – to people with no incomes, no job and no assets – look in retrospect to have been criminally irresponsible. But at the time it seemed a worthy idea, as in the UK, to spread the fruits of home ownership from the middle class to poor Americans, often recent immigrants or poor black people, as part of a process of empowerment and liberation from the ghetto or from poor-quality public housing. And, as in Britain, property seemed self-evidently a good investment, as house prices doubled in value from the late 1990s to the peak in 2006, out-performing the stock exchange by a considerable distance over that period.

More-cynical observers might ask why bankers suddenly became so enthusiastic about poor people whom they otherwise wouldn't have touched with a financial bargepole, and certainly wouldn't want in their golf clubs. Philanthropy can be discounted. Poor people have one great attraction. Because they are poor, and have a poor credit history, they can be charged relatively high interest rates. Of course, this was not obvious to the borrowers, who were offered low-interest 'teaser rates', which would then be refinanced later at a higher rate. For banks looking for new business with a high yield the attractions were obvious, especially if they could find a way of spreading the (higher) risk. An instrument to achieve just that was at hand in the form of collateralized debt obligations (CDOs), or packages of debt paying interest rates that varied according to the risk. These could be sold as bonds in international markets. Soon, mortgage-backed securities accounted for a third of the whole US $27 trillion bond market – and of this, at the end of 2007, $1.3 trillion was sub-prime. The concept of 'sub-prime' is an elastic one, but the USA, unlike the UK, has a formal definition based on the multiple of borrower's income and loan value relative to house acquisition price.

So far, so good. Lots of poor people (and others) were able to buy their homes for the first time when interest rates were low and house prices were rising. Lots of happy bankers and brokers were paid bonuses for successfully closing deals. Lots of pensioners and other investors across the world were enjoying a higher yield on the securities that made up the assets of the institutions to which they had entrusted their money.

What burst the bubble of US property values was rising interest rates. The US equivalent of the bank rate rose from 1 per cent to over 5 per cent in early 2006. Large numbers of borrowers could no longer afford to pay. Many of the sub-prime borrowers gave up when their 'teaser' loans at low interest were refinanced at the new, higher rate. Large numbers simply handed over their keys to their bank and disappeared, not waiting to be repossessed. The market fell sharply, with distress-selling as the bubble burst. Prices fell on average by 25 per cent from the peak in July 2006 to the autumn of 2008; and derivatives markets, which enable investors to bet on future movements in prices, predict a comparable fall still to come. The number of potential repossessions has been variously estimated at 2 million on the conservative side to as many as 6.5 million by Credit Suisse – as many as one in ten mortgages.

Whilst this story was distressing for those American families, it is not immediately obvious why their problems should have reverberated around the world. To understand this, I need to explain how the US mortgage market works and how its risks are transmitted to wider financial markets. The total US mortgage market was worth roughly $12 trillion in July 2008. This sum compared then with a UK mortgage market of $2.5 trillion (or £1.2 trillion) – five times smaller. US mortgage lenders, who are far more numerous than in the UK, raise money for new loans by selling on their debt to other institutions. Of the total $12 trillion, $5.2 trillion was acquired, and effectively guaranteed (or so it was assumed at the time), by two state-backed but privately owned agencies, the Federal Home Loan Mortgage Corporation, known as 'Freddie Mac', and the Federal National Mortgage Association, known as 'Fannie Mae'. Fannie Mae had been created during the New Deal as a way of stimulating, while also stabilizing, mortgage lending and, thereby, the housing industry. In 1968 it was privatized, to help finance the Vietnam War, and its explicit guarantee was dropped, while Freddie Mac was set up as a competitor. These two agencies became the stalwarts of the Middle American mortgage market, buying and selling mortgages below a certain size (just over $400,000), but not the riskier sub-prime mortgages. Those were left to the (fully) private-sector banks, which advanced a mixture of high-grade, high-value and sub-prime mortgages. While Fannie Mae and Freddie Mac did not support sub-prime lending directly – though they had a lot of marginally prime loans – they did, however, hold large amounts of securities backed by sub-prime mortgages, so they were, indirectly, highly exposed to that market.

Freddie Mac and Fannie Mae, and the banks, then sought to sell on the mortgage debt they had acquired in the form of mortgage-backed securities. This process of securitization broadened out into a slicing and dicing of the risks, through an exotic proliferation of new instruments, including the aforementioned CDOs and SIVs (special investment vehicles). By repackaging the mortgage debt through more and more complex vehicles, securitization made it possible to dilute and spread the risk, gain access to a wider pool of capital, and thus reduce the cost of borrowing. At the same time, securitization provided investors with new products to invest in at a competitive yield.

This relatively small amount of debt was leveraged with much larger amounts of debt. In practice, each transaction could generate a margin of profit from which the managers of the institutions and their shareholders, brokers, dealers, rating agencies, designers of asset packages, sales staff and lawyers could all take their cut. The degree of leverage involved also amplified the debt, sometimes to astronomical proportions. In effect, institutions borrowed money in order to buy debt, which was the security for the borrowing, and the money they borrowed was in turn borrowed, sometimes through several institutions. In addition, debt default could be insured against, but the insurers depended in turn on borrowed capital. Derivatives markets also made it possible to hedge (or speculate) against the risk of default. The credit default swap market, for example, which grew on the back of the growth of these debt instruments, achieved a notional value of over $60 trillion. This, in turn, represented about one tenth of the overall size of derivatives markets, which Warren Buffet warned us was the H-bomb to follow the sub-prime A-bomb.

How has the downturn in the US housing market, and increase in mortgage default, had such a profound impact on financial markets, triggering panic among the sophisticated financiers who thought they had diluted the toxicity of sub-prime loans to harmless levels? At first sight, the sums of money involved in sub-prime losses simply do not justify the collapse of confidence that has occurred. Let us assume, for the sake of illustration, that roughly one third of the total US sub-prime debt eventually has to be written off by the financial institutions that hold it: that is, around $400 billion. Perhaps this overstates the problem, since the earlier sub-prime loans, before 2005, seem to have held up well. The sum is less than the losses in the 1980s savings and loans crisis, even in nominal terms. It represents only 3 per cent of total mortgage debt. In fact, when the IMF made its estimate of total US financial sector losses in its Global Financial Stability Report, it estimated that, of total losses of $1.4 trillion ($1400 billion), only around $150 billion could be traced to mortgages, and only a fraction of that to sub-prime mortgages. So much for the idea that US sub-prime lending caused the crisis. It was merely the fuse that lit the bomb. The explosive was non-traditional lending outside the banking system, centring on securitization. Through securitization, loans once held on the books of banks were repackaged and sold. The scale and complexity of this repackaging increased many times in the rapidly growing pool of debt-based products created by investment banks.

The genius of securitization is also its central weakness. Debt is so widely and skilfully diffused that it becomes impossible to trace it. No one really owns the loans. So institutions have struggled to identify how much their own financial assets, backed by sub-prime mortgages, are actually worth, and how much should be written down. A yet more serious problem is what are called 'amplifiers', multiplying losses (and gains) and adding to uncertainty. Amplification of losses has come from several sources, the most important being excessive leverage. Banks, and particularly investment banks, increased borrowing relative to equity (share capital) in order to achieve higher returns for shareholders' equity when the value of assets was rising. In a world where investors were seeking higher returns on their assets, one recourse, which occurred here on a grand scale, was to assume more and more debt in order to buy assets, thus pushing up their value further, but increasing risk in the process.

The investment banks were at the heart of this process of increasing leverage. Leverage of 30:1 was not uncommon. The bankers were able, for a while, to make large profits from a big expansion of business on small underlying assets, with each financial instrument created becoming collateral for yet more complex instruments. Furthermore, some of the debt instruments, such as CDOs, produced substantial profits from small increases in asset values – but, conversely, multiplied losses once asset values fell.

Other amplifiers have included derivatives, which involve contracts at one stage removed from the original transaction. In some form they have been around since organized commerce began, and they perform the useful function of enabling traders to cover themselves against future changes in prices (and financiers to make money by selling that cover). For those owning a derivative, the contract creates exposure to risk, even if the underlying assets are not actually owned. Derivatives have grown at a staggering rate in today's sophisticated markets, to an estimated notional value of outstanding contracts of $600 trillion (from $15 trillion a decade earlier) at the end of 2007 – over ten times world output. One particular kind of derivative, credit default swaps (CDS), which allow investors to separate out – and pay for – the risk that a borrower will not repay, have been crucial to the growth of financial leverage. This $60 trillion market (which has grown from virtually zero in a little over five years) permits, in effect, gambling at very long odds that banks and other institutions, including governments, will not fail. Bookies at the racecourse carefully adjust the odds in order to ensure that they reflect the backing of different horses. They, like casino owners, know from experience and intuitive maths not to put their firm or their house at risk. But the novelty and complex maths of the CDS market has meant that large bets have been advanced – usually in borrowed money – which are cumulatively so vast that there is no underlying capacity to pay out in the event of their being called in. And that is the weakness that was exposed when a large bank such as Lehman Brothers did indeed default on its debts.

Taking all the amplification into account, US losses from the current crisis were estimated by the IMF in the autumn of 2008 at around $1.4 trillion, 7 per cent of US GDP and fifty or more times larger than the sub-prime losses. But these estimates of losses are but a fraction of the losses that will eventually come as recession takes further toll and a process of deleveraging takes place, with assets being offloaded at distress prices.

A succession of events occurred in the early months of 2007 that, to the acute observer at the time, and more clearly in retrospect, could be seen as the early warnings of the storm to come. In February, specialist US sub-prime lenders were reporting losses on the back of defaults, and the second-largest, New Century, was suspended and then filed for bankruptcy. Then, in May, UBS was forced to take over its in-house hedge fund, Dillon Read, which had run up heavy losses in sub-prime investment, and shortly afterwards UBS's chief executive was fired. In June, two hedge funds run by Bear Stearns were reputed to be in serious trouble, despite having supposedly very safe investments, because they were exposed to bonds backed by sub-prime mortgage debt.

It was becoming clear, in mid-2007, that serious losses were accruing from the sub-prime market and the wider fall in house prices, and that these losses were being transmitted through the system. Banks became nervous about the underlying value of their assets. They therefore hoarded cash and cut back drastically on their lending. Moreover, banks could no longer attract funding from money markets worried about the underlying health of their borrowers. Liquidity dried up. There was a crisis of confidence in complex securities run by BNP–Paribas, and a bail-out by the banks of a German bank, IKB. Then came the run on Northern Rock. But even banks with adequate liquidity gradually had to acknowledge that many of their assets were of diminished value. Citigroup wrote down $41 billion in the period from January 2007 to the end of June 2008; UBS (Union de Banques Suisses), a Swiss-owned global giant, and Merrill Lynch each wrote down almost $40 billion, and the UK's Royal Bank of Scotland $16 billion. Share values of the world's largest banks, UBS and Citicorp, fell 50 per cent in the year up to May 2008.

———

The impact of these changes on the world outside banking has been felt through the slow, quiet strangulation of bank lending to those institutions or markets that are now seen as excessively risky. In the UK, for example, 40 per cent of new mortgages depended, until the credit crunch, on international credit markets, which have effectively closed. It could be argued that such a radical reassessment of risk is, on balance, healthy. Too much money was flowing into mortgages, especially but not only sub-prime mortgages, driving up house prices to a level that represented an artificially inflated bubble. And it is sensible that this process should go into reverse, even if the contraction is painful. A more realistic pricing of risk should, in principle, still leave plenty of opportunities for good companies and households to borrow. The worry is, however, that even such healthy lending has been choked off, and that the process of adjustment to more-prudent lending is happening so rapidly and brutally that it is causing severe economic contraction and much harm to good as well as to high-risk borrowers.

Several events over the last year have reinforced the pessimistic view that the process of deleveraging from excessive debt is so painful and difficult that it can no longer be left to the financial markets to sort it out. On Friday, 14 March 2008, the Federal Reserve, with the support of the federal government, rescued Bear Stearns from bankruptcy. Bear Stearns had seriously over-extended itself in risky securitized markets and was on the brink of collapse. The judgement was made that its collapse would have widespread systemic impact, dragging down other institutions. In particular, Bear Stearns was counter-party to a staggering $10 trillion of swaps through its derivatives activities. Were these claims to escalate from the hypothetical to the actual there would have been a further draining of liquidity and large balance-sheet losses, threatening insolvency to institutions holding the now devalued paper. The Fed acted as 'lender of last resort'. This was the first time that an investment bank had been treated in this way, reflecting the fact that investment banks are no longer specialist, niche institutions but have become integral to the financial system. Bear Stearns's shareholders were hit badly during the rescue operation, but salvaged $1 billion, a tenth of the bank's value prior to the collapse. Taxpayers assumed responsibility in the form of a $29 billion credit line to support a bundle of (the worst) mortgage assets, enabling a takeover of Bear Stearns by JPMorgan Chase to go ahead at a knock-down price.

Problems followed elsewhere on an almost daily basis. Two large US banks, Washington Mutual and Wachovia, sacked their top management as reports spread that they were in difficulties. Another class of institutions – the 'monolines', which give insurance for credit – were in difficulties, as MBIA and Ambac had their ratings downgraded. The intervention to rescue Bear Stearns had initially reduced the perceived risk of credit default of major banks and therefore the risk of insuring against default. But subsequently the cost of insurance rose again sharply, hitting the monolines. The problems of the insurers fed into Freddie Mac and Fannie Mae, which relied on a healthy insurance industry to cover their own losses.

Then, on 7 July, it was reported that Fannie Mae and Freddie Mac would have to raise an extra $75 billion to cover losses on their sub-prime-backed securities and dodgier loans. Shares in the two companies fell heavily as doubts spread as to who would cover these losses, and how. Since the companies were highly leveraged with vast debt and little equity, there was little reserve capital within the institutions themselves. These institutions mattered enormously, since, following the impact of the credit crunch on the banks, they were almost the only bodies providing credit to the US mortgage market, where they already provided most of the mortgage finance to middle-class Americans, albeit at a subsidy. Their debts were also massive: $5.3 trillion in debt and credit obligations, equivalent to the entire publicly held debt of the US government. This fitted the description of 'too big to fail'.

The federal government therefore decided that it had no alternative but to support the beleaguered companies, and offered what amounted to unlimited loans. The government provided an explicit guarantee instead of an implicit one, worth between $122 and $182 billion on one estimate. Then, on 11 July, another substantial bank, Indy Mac Bankcorp, had its assets taken over by the bank regulator when its depositors panicked and started queuing for cash. Two weeks later, two regional banks, from Nevada and California, were taken over.

A downward spiral, or 'toxic loop', was setting in. Anxiety about the banks meant that their costs for borrowing became higher than for non-financial companies, making bank lending unprofitable. Then, banks were obliged to take back on to their balance sheets previous securitizations from insurance companies and pension funds, some with big losses. Furthermore, as they tried to raise capital in order to meet their reserve requirements, they were forced to sell assets, thus driving down their prices, especially as it became difficult to raise more capital from share-holders, who had become thoroughly scared. And as the economic downturn intensified, with more defaults in mortgages, there were more losses and more pain, and confidence ebbed further. In the quarter to the end of June 2008, US bank loans were contracting at an annual rate of 8 per cent. A similar process was taking place in the UK.

These events were, however, merely the eddies that preceded the eye of the storm that hit Wall Street in the second week of September. The explicit guarantees to Fannie Mae and Freddie Mac proved inadequate to prevent a loss of confidence, reflected in collapsing share values. The two institutions, which provide 80 per cent of US mortgages, were deemed too big to fail and were nationalized. The US state formally acquired institutions with assets of $1.8 trillion, wiping out their shareholders. Nationalization formalized de facto state control. This was a striking event for an administration with an evangelical belief in private-enterprise capitalism.

Then there was a collapse of confidence in Lehman Brothers, a venerable 158-year-old institution and the fourth-largest investment bank in the USA. The US administration made the crucial decision to let it go bankrupt and not to help Barclays take it over as a going concern. After rescuing Bear Stearns several months earlier, the decision was a carefully – if rapidly – calculated gamble that the bank was insolvent and not merely illiquid, and that the failure of the bank would not result in widespread systemic failure. The risk was a big one, since Lehman's had a major role as counter-party in the credit derivatives market, and critics have argued ever since that it should have been rescued. After the powerful signal that the government would not automatically bail out investment banks, Merrill Lynch, which was also in trouble, sold out to the Bank of America for $50 billion, a tiny fraction of its pre-crisis value.

An even more dramatic intervention led to the state takeover of the world's largest insurer, AIG, with an $85 billion loan. A small section of AIG had, independently, and perhaps without the knowledge of the insurance managers, succeeded in taking on $450 billion of credit default swaps. Had the company been allowed to collapse, it would not only have dragged down large chunks of the global insurance markets – grounding a high proportion of the world's commercial aircraft – but would have had a massive impact on banks and investment funds. Nationalization was seen as a lesser evil than letting AIG collapse.

It soon became clear that financial markets were in a state of blind, uncontrolled panic. Contagion could be seen in many areas: a collapse in bank shares, allegedly fuelled by short-selling (that is, speculation by means of selling borrowed shares); a leap in the cost of insuring against bank default; and the growing cost of borrowing because of an increase in the cost of banks lending to one another. There was a flight to safe assets, notably government bonds, reflected in negative interest rates on US Treasury Bills (that is, investors were willing to lose money on lending to the government rather than lend to commercial money markets or banks). The panic was spreading well beyond the USA. In the UK, Bradford & Bingley collapsed and was nationalized. Halifax–Bank of Scotland (HBOS) was heading the same way, had Lloyds TSB not launched a $22 billion takeover. The crisis was reaching a critical stage. The situation was deteriorating by the day and was approaching the point at which investors were no longer willing to trust banks overnight. This is the point at which the whole financial system was close to total collapse – leading, potentially, to an economy dependent on barter. In previous generations that crisis point would have led to a run on the banks by depositors; but, apart from a nervy weekend when Ireland offered all its depositors unconditional guarantees, there was a common-sense understanding (helped by earlier interventions, such as the nationalization of Northern Rock in the UK and AIG in the USA) that, whatever happened, depositors would be protected. It was clear, though, that piecemeal action was no longer enough and that a comprehensive, and coordinated, approach was required.

A key step was to recognize – based on long-established, nineteenth-century practice – that banks should have whatever liquidity is necessary from the central bank (albeit at a penalty rate and secured against sound collateral). In an effort to prevent a crippling squeeze in credit the US administration pumped $180 billion into money markets to offset the hoarding of cash by frightened institutions, and other central banks followed. Short-selling was banned so as to take the immediate pressure off bank shares; short-selling had been threatening the system by driving down bank shares to the point of disabling the banks' ability to raise capital themselves.

But the crucial step was the recognition that, if the banks were to return to their central role as financial intermediaries, they would need help in adjusting to the large losses that they had made. Writing off losses required capital. Capital could no longer be raised, unaided, from the markets through the normal mechanism of rights issues to shareholders, and new sources of capital (such as sovereign wealth funds) were wary or very expensive. There was a danger that banks would try to realize capital by drastically cutting their lending, with profoundly damaging effects on the real economy (or else try to conceal the problem, as the Japanese banks had done in the 1990s, which would perpetuate the lack of confidence). The issue, then, was how best to help restore the banks' balance sheets to health.

The first attempt to grapple with this problem was the Paulson plan in the USA, to set up a fund of $700 billion to buy up 'toxic' mortgage-related securities from the banks. It soon became clear that market confidence generally – as reflected in a highly volatile and collapsing stock market – hinged on getting the plan accepted by Congress. It was, however, a badly conceived and politically unpopular plan. If the purchases of bad debts were at current market prices, there would be no relief. If they were on more generous terms, then the banks were being bailed out without any obvious benefit to the taxpayer, and irresponsible lenders were being rewarded. Nor was there any guarantee that the buy-out programme would make more than a marginal impact. There were, in addition, many practical questions about how the mechanism would work. Congress baulked at the package and, at the first time of asking, rejected it, fuelling ever more uncertainty. A compromise proposal was then passed, with some protection for the taxpayer, and the hope was that if toxic debt could be valued – notwithstanding its considerable complexity – this would create a liquid market for mortgage-backed securities. Once that happened losses could be valued and written down in an orderly way.

At this key moment, however, the UK government came up with an alternative proposal for injecting money into the banks more quickly, by advancing capital directly through a form of partial nationalization. The state agreed to invest £37 billion in leading banks that sought funding to repair their balance sheet in ordinary and preference shares, resulting in the de facto nationalization of Royal Bank of Scotland/NatWest and HBOS, and a minority stake in Lloyds TSB. The state preference shares enjoy a 12 per cent interest for taxpayers who receive no dividends on the ordinary shares. Other than the interest rate, the main attraction for the taxpayer is that the banks have agreed to a (rather vague) undertaking to maintain lending and to restrain bonus payments. The UK package is based on a similar strategy to that which was adopted in Sweden in the early 1990s to resolve a banking crisis following a property bubble. The Swedish approach was more far-reaching: there was a guarantee for all deposits and creditors; and there was a mechanism for separating out bad debts. But it succeeded in stabilizing the banking system, and the government made money from the subsequent share sell-off.

The British plan for recapitalization was both more direct and more urgent than the Paulson plan and was quickly adopted as a framework for intervention in the G7 countries. It was also accompanied by measures to guarantee inter-bank lending. The package, particularly when adopted by other developed countries and accompanied by parallel measures such as a concerted cut in interest rates, helped to stabilize the position, at least in the short term, though inter-bank lending remained sluggish.

It had become clear by the New Year however that, although the banking system had been saved from immediate collapse, it remained in desperate straits, requiring continued intervention. In the USA, Bank of America had to be rescued and Citigroup was broken up. The Irish government nationalized Anglo-Irish. The Commerzbank was rescued in Germany. The British government launched a scheme to provide guarantees for new business lending and set out the broad framework of a programme to insure the banks' bad debts. Investors were not impressed; shares fell drastically in RBS/NatWest, Lloyds/HBOS and Barclays in anticipation of nationalization.

At the time of writing it was not clear whether the new US and UK interventions would be sufficient to stimulate lending to solvent borrowers, or whether the process of deleveraging would lead to further tightening of credit as banks and other institutions hung on to capital, leading to deepening recession. This could create more default in corporate debt, on mortgages, credit cards, car loans and commercial property. This in turn would create more bad debt and more reason for banks to hoard capital rather than lend it. It is easy to see how such a downward spiral could lead to a deepening slump. Ominously, the US authorities abandoned the Paulson plan as unworkable, and it was clear that in the UK the banks were taking little notice of any undertaking to maintain lending. Nationalization loomed.

There is, therefore, as yet no sign of a reversal of the contraction in lending – which is also what occurred in the 'great contraction' from 1929 to 1932. It is precisely because of the institutional memory of that disaster that the pressure has mounted on the authorities to offset the deflationary risk. Deflation arises because firms slash prices, and wages, in order to survive. However, consumers, expecting still further price cuts, hold back from spending, thus worsening the outlook for companies even further and forcing down prices, in a downward spiral. Pre-war experience suggests that it then becomes essential, in this unusual set of conditions, to provide a monetary stimulus by cutting interest rates, and a fiscal stimulus by, temporarily, running a larger budget deficit than would normally occur even in a downturn.

Until just recently, all the major developed countries' central banks have been trying to balance inflationary against deflationary risk. Their assessment of risk has been heavily influenced by history. The approach of the Federal Reserve is dominated by lessons learned from the 1930s; that of the European Central Bank by memories of hyperinflation; and that of the UK by recent experience of inflationary wage–price spirals. The USA, like Europe, had good reason to worry about inflationary risk, since consumer price index (CPI) inflation had recently passed 5 per cent and inflation expectations, as measured by survey data and by the gap between real and normal bond yields, suggested until an advanced stage of the crisis that inflation would increase.

To set alongside these concerns, however, was the growing worry that a credit squeeze would hit spending and growth; that a falling housing market would depress the sense of well-being and willingness to spend; and that unemployment would add to housing market defaults and overall lack of confidence. Deflation was thus becoming a greater risk than inflation, and were deflation to take hold it would increase the real cost of debt and make the drag of debt on the economy all the more severe. By November 2008 it was clear to the US and UK authorities – and even to the more reluctant European Central Bank – that interest rates should be cut drastically. The possibility of zero or near-zero interest rates loomed large.

The links between the credit crunch and the real economy are difficult to trace with any confidence, and there are still those who argue that the financial markets' preoccupation with deleveraging has little connection with real people in the real world. It has been described as akin to betting at a horse race: fascinating for punters and bookies, but with no bearing on the actual race. The US authorities, however, are not so insouciant, and their sense of alarm has dominated policy, and particularly monetary policy. There was an aggressive cut in Federal Reserve Funds interest rates, from 5.25 to 2 per cent, at the onset of the crisis, almost as radical and more abrupt than the cut from 6.5 to 1 per cent in response to the perceived threat in the 2000–1 period. The Bush administration and Congress, between them, have also contrived a massive 'Keynesian' budget deficit – turning a budget surplus of 4 per cent of GDP in 2000, and an expected surplus of 4.5 per cent in 2005 in the absence of any policy change, into a deficit of 2.5–3 per cent of GDP expected in 2008, and probably well over 5 per cent in 2009. In the UK, as we saw in the last chapter, the government has also made the case for 'reflationary' policy in order to stave off the expected contraction in demand, production and employment that could result from financial institutions retreating too rapidly from their function of providing credit to the real economy. There are those who worry that governments are acting precipitately, however, and risk creating even bigger problems in the future.

These reservations expose a deep dividing line in policy. In fact, the financial crisis has thrown up two major, related sets of controversies, which expose fundamental fault lines in economic and political thinking. One is how far governments should intervene to stop panics and financial crises, by acting as lender of last resort, rather than letting them run their course. The second is whether, in the aftermath of the excesses of the financial crisis, there should be a reversion to tighter regulation of markets, and, if so, in what form.

————

The first issue – whether the authorities should intervene in a financial crisis – is one that has preoccupied policy makers ever since what Kindleberger calls 'speculative manias' have been recorded. These go back to the bubble in tulips, Dutch East India Company shares and other financial excesses of Holland in the 1630s, or the *Kipper- und Wipperzeit* wave of speculation in coinage among the German princely states a little earlier. From the outset, but particularly with the emergence of economic theory in eighteenth-century Britain and France, there has been a gulf between those who worried about moral hazard – the rewarding of imprudence, greed and folly – and those who worried that financial panics would spread and infect the real economy. The former view was most succinctly summed up by Herbert Spencer: 'The ultimate result of shielding man from the effects of folly is to people the world with fools.' This approach was influential in the years of the Great Crash, and it helped inform the advice given to President Hoover by his Treasury Secretary, Andrew Mellon: to do nothing. '[Panic] will purge the rottenness out of the system ... People will work harder and live a more moral life ... enterprising people will pick up the wrecks from less competent people.' Since Hoover and Mellon emerged as the fools who precipitated the Great Depression, their abstemiousness became seriously unfashionable.

The theory of moral hazard has been invoked more recently by the Governor of the Bank of England, Mervyn King, in initially resisting a bail-out of Northern Rock. His has been a more sophisticated version of the argument than Mellon's, based less on self-righteousness and a desire to punish the imprudent than a practical concern that free insurance or underwriting from the government would encourage further excessive risk-taking. The experience of the Greenspan years was that if the US Federal Reserve intervened quickly to cut interest rates drastically at any sign of a potential financial crisis, it would lead to a new wave of imprudent investment behaviour when the economy recovered. Financiers came to accept such intervention as normal, and as a duty of government.

This view was put, in parody form, by a leading US hedge-fund manager, Jim Cramer, who lost his temper on CNBC television when the financial storm broke in August 2007, accusing the Federal Reserve of being 'asleep' and Mr Bernanke of 'behaving like an academic', and demanding help for 'my people' (that is to say, Wall Street). Much more abuse of the same kind was directed at Mervyn King in London for not opening his cheque book sooner.

In practice, in the early nineteenth century an approach to financial crises was developed pragmatically, by trial and error, and was later rationalized by Walter Bagehot. The resulting rule was that it is the job of central banks to advance liquidity to other banks when required, but only at a penalty rate, against sound collateral, and not to institutions that are insolvent. A procedure developed about two hundred years ago, and crystallized 130 years ago, has survived remarkably well the big changes that have subsequently taken place in banking. But there is much scope for misunderstanding over what the rule means in practice, since suitable collateral is a matter for judgement and the distinction between solvency and illiquidity can be less than clear.

Financial commentators and financiers unfavourably contrasted the reluctance of the Bank of England to assist banks during the crisis of August 2008 with the greater willingness of the European Central Bank and the Federal Reserve. The Bank of England took a less accommodating approach to collateral; it was, understandably, reluctant to accept mortgages on taxpayers' behalf in a falling housing market. But there was a more fundamental point. Mervyn King, in a comment that was to create a serious hostage to fortune, gave a classic statement of the case against indulging moral hazard a few days before the rescue of Northern Rock: 'The provision of large liquidity facilities penalizes those financial institutions that sat out the dance, encourages herd behaviour and increases the intensity of future crises.' Not only did the Governor then have to acquiesce in the rescue operation for Northern Rock, but several months later opened a special liquidity facility from which bankers could borrow, albeit with a penalty. The European Central Bank, by contrast, appears to be willing to lend as and when required, without a penalty rate. And after Mr Cramer's tantrum was taken to heart, the Federal Reserve was enthusiastically praised by Wall Street. Perhaps that was because it did what was asked of it, and in its later rescue of Bear Stearns, and then Freddie Mac and Fannie Mae, went beyond the traditional role of lender of last resort by rescuing companies from threatened insolvency.

The three main central banks affected by the crisis have carried out their classic lender of last resort liquidity functions with varying enthusiasm and alacrity. There has been less common ground, and greater divergence, in the practical meaning of moral hazard in respect of rescue operations for failing institutions. As we noted above, when the Bear Stearns operation took place, the Federal Reserve acted speedily, through a guaranteed line of credit, to ensure that the bank was taken over, by JPMorgan Chase. The US authorities were less interested in the long-term risks of moral hazard than in the immediate consequences of bankruptcy triggering widespread default on the banks' obligations in respect of derivatives. The state partially stabilized some of the risks of future losses. The shareholders were reprieved; instead of losing their shirts, they were allowed to retain roughly $1 billion in value. JPMorgan Chase, which took over the bank, had an opportunity to profit from any recovery, while benefiting from taxpayer guarantees, the full magnitude of which is not clear.

Those who felt queasy about this use of the economic muscle of the state to support supposedly risk-taking, profit-seeking firms had even more reason to worry about the rescue of Fannie Mae and Freddie Mac. These privately owned bodies were given limitless state guarantees. No change was demanded in a management team whose business model, reinforced by personal incentives, had created excessive risk. And there were continued dividends for shareholders, who had already benefited substantially from earlier implicit government guarantees.

It was only after a time lag of two months and a further bout of uncertainty in the markets that the US authorities introduced a new set of controls over the private institutions they had rescued. The US authorities gave ample demonstration of Martin Luther King's description of his country's approach to policy half a century ago: 'socialism for the rich and rugged free-market capitalism for the poor'. It was primarily a belated anxiety about moral hazard that then persuaded the US authorities to let Lehman Brothers go bankrupt, rather than to rescue it like Bear Stearns. Yet the later Paulson plan was full of moral hazard – taxpayers offering to take over the bad debts of the most irresponsible banks.

The alternative approach to rescue involves securing gains for the taxpayer, and avoiding moral hazard, by nationalizing failing institutions, replacing their management, and then selling them on in improved economic conditions, without rewards for the investors whose institutions had failed. The US had employed this approach in the past, with the Continental Illinois Bank in 1984. More systematically, it was used by Sweden and other Scandinavian authorities in the early 1990s, as we have already noted. There was a major banking crisis costing the economy 6 per cent of GDP between 1990 and 1993, which was dealt with by a mixture of bank closures, government-sponsored reconstruction, and temporary nationalization under the direction of a Bank Support Authority.

Britain has finished up in a similar place to the Swedes. It first struggled with the problem of Northern Rock, nationalizing it, but only after months of indecision. The initial hope was a Bear Stearns-type rescue by Lloyds, involving a £25 billion government guarantee. It was never clear, however, what the terms of such a deal were and particularly how the risks and losses, or potential profits, were to be allocated between the government and the private sector. For several months the government sought, in the full glare of publicity, to effect another private sale, to Richard Branson or other potential buyers. But the same set of problems proved insurmountable: how to ensure that the risks to the government of continued loans and guarantees would be properly offset by appropriate rewards; that the new private owners would share properly in the risks; and that current shareholders would not profit from government guarantees. The government also indulged for far too long the odd notion that the Northern Rock management had made no mistakes and were therefore part of the solution. When the banking crisis struck with full intensity in the autumn of 2008 lessons had been learned, and when it was decided that Bradford & Bingley had to be rescued, it was nationalized promptly.

Some lessons have been learned from these contrasting experiences about how to reconcile rescue operations designed to preserve financial stability with the avoidance of moral hazard. Nationalization is one route, though there are other ways of striking a proper balance, through strict conditions for rescues: upper limits on assistance; drastic reorganization; removal and, if necessary, punishment of existing management; penalty rates on credit; a freeze on dividends during the lifetime of a rescue; guarantees for the government of participating in the potential upside. The British recapitalization plan was of this kind though the conditions turn out to have been largely token. The rescue victim might baulk at such conditions – and they have – in which case the government has the option of nationalization. Seen in this way, far from temporary nationalization being a step towards socialism, it is an essential tool for managing a market economy and maintaining its disciplines in a financial crisis.

Questions of moral hazard do not stop at institutions and shareholders. They also affect depositors, the millions of individuals whose savings form the basis of the banking system. The dilemma is this: if depositors fear that they might lose their money if they leave it in a bank, they will incline towards safer but less productive options, such as hiding it under the bed, buying gold and jewellery or land, or spending it. But if they are fully protected from the risk of losing their money they may flock to banks that offer higher returns by cutting corners and taking excessive risks. There is a tricky balance to be struck. The trickiness is made more difficult by the fact that banking is inherently risky and rests ultimately on the hope that depositors will not all ask for their money back at the same time, since most of it is tied up in illiquid assets.

The key turning point in depositor protection was in the 1930s. Prior to that banks, by and large, depended on their reputations. Financially conservative banks attracted depositors through periods of financial turbulence precisely because they were, or claimed to be, very cautious in their use of savings, investing heavily in government paper or businesses with good collateral. In the UK, reputation has also been the mainstay of a system that rested, at least for the last century, on a small number of large banks that had never seen a run by their depositors. The USA, however, had a somewhat more freewheeling system in which banks occasionally sank and savers drowned with them. The Great Crash led to the biggest bank run in history and in turn to the establishment of deposit guarantees operated by the Federal Deposit Insurance Corporation. These initially covered deposits of $10,000, which was later raised to $100,000. The FDIC financed its operations by collecting premiums from banks, which passed on the cost to their customers. The FDIC had plenty of practice, mostly with tiny banks, and it worked well in stopping runs. It ran into two difficulties, however. One was that when a really big bank failed – like Continental Illinois in 1984 and First Republic Bank of Dallas in 1988 – it felt obliged to abandon the upper limit in order to prevent panic. The other was that its purposes (and those of sister institutions) became subverted by their being given a central role in rescuing banks, as opposed to their depositors, using taxpayers' money.

By contrast, European post-war banking systems have been tightly controlled and, in some countries, nationalized, partly in response to the banking disasters of the 1930s. So issues of depositor protection have been less in evidence than in the USA. In the UK there was the additional protection of informal guarantees between the banks, which were formalized in 1890 when Barings

Bank capsized and others, such as Martins, were threatened. There was also a post-war system of depositor protection – insuring deposits up to £35,000 – but it was hardly used, largely because the high-street banks were assumed to be totally reliable (and protected, as institutions, by the mysterious but seemingly definitive lender of last resort role of the authorities). Those portentous bank branches that dominated the high street, and which used to be inhabited by smartly dressed, socially superior staff, overseen by a terrifying manager, were the embodiment of reliability. It was a privilege to be allowed to bank there and, even more, to borrow. Depositors could sleep safely knowing that improvident riff-raff were being kept at bay and that the army of bean-counters knew how to add up.

Mrs Thatcher's financial reforms of the 1980s radically changed the high-street banks from being safe but boring to being more aggressively competitive – but also, we have discovered, less secure. In particular, they competed to offer loans on attractive terms. The credit card revolution further liberalized lending. The proliferation of banks in the 1990s, with the demutualization of UK building societies, added to competition. Perhaps someone in the Bank of England or the Treasury should have stopped to think about 'what if' scenarios, such as the risk of a small but ambitious bank behaving recklessly and putting its depositors at risk. But no one did. Until Northern Rock. It soon became clear that very few of Northern Rock's depositors knew that they were protected or, if they did know, did not trust the system to pay up (they were right, in the sense that the process is cumbersome and takes months). They panicked, and Britain suffered the first bank run for over a century. It was only stopped by the Chancellor offering unlimited guarantees to depositors (as the US authorities had done in the 1980s to head off the run on Continental Illinois).

A sense of panic resurfaced in the middle of the September–October 2008 banking crisis when Ireland sought to prevent a run on its banks by offering unconditional guarantees, leading Greece and some other European countries to follow suit. The

UK came close to being forced to follow, but a combination of the reassurance (for depositors) of nationalization as a last resort and a depositor protection scheme (now being improved by parliament) prevented further panic. Even private depositors in the risky but high yielding Icelandic banks were fully protected (but not councils or charities).

There is one further dimension to moral hazard and the risks of banking, which concerns the borrower. Few would dispute the general proposition that, if people borrow money, they have a responsibility to repay; and if they offer security, then that security is forfeit in the event of default. There are a lot of questions about lending practices, particularly in respect of sub-prime loans, and on mis-selling and the aggressive promotion of debt. But this is essentially an issue of the regulation of lending practices. Few would advocate large-scale debt waivers, since the moral hazard in encouraging future excessive borrowing is obvious. Recent changes in bankruptcy laws in the UK may, indeed, have encouraged such behaviour. There is, however, at the heart of current policy a big issue of moral hazard in relation to borrowers. By slashing interest rates, governments and central banks are rewarding borrowers and penalizing thrifty depositors. If current policy leads to inflation, then the effect will be compounded. The economic expediency of expansionary policy has to be weighed against the danger of perverse rewards.

There is a particular problem with mortgage debt, since calling in collateral means home repossession. This is not merely distressing for the families concerned, but can involve – in the UK, though less so in the US – an obligation on the public authorities to rehouse them. Repossession ('foreclosure' in America) is also a very costly process, and imposes costs on the home owners if the process of auctioning or distress-selling drives down prices. Public policy has to address the issue of borrowers who are willing and eager but temporarily unable to pay. In the UK, it is possible, with conditions and qualifications, to obtain help with mortgage payments through social security. There is also a reasonable concern that the taxpayer should not shoulder all the obligations of the borrower and the risks of the lender. Payment protection insurance is another option, but, unless compulsory, will only be taken up by small numbers since policies are costly and/or their cover heavily qualified.

What is needed, to avoid large-scale and unnecessary repossession, is for negotiated compromises in the event that payments are missed, rather than the automatic triggering of legal action. In the UK the Council of Mortgage Lenders has a code of conduct which requires lenders to offer a range of alternatives to try to keep families in their homes. Making such a voluntary code binding on all lenders, including the 'free-riders', would be a useful step, and the government has now moved in that direction. In the USA, there are proposals before Congress to modify bankruptcy law and to reapportion losses more equitably between creditor and debtor. As the repossession crisis grows in the USA and the UK, there will be growing pressure for the state either to assume some of the risks and costs or to intervene to protect the borrower.

———

Banking is an Alice in Wonderland world, in which financiers earn high salaries for taking and covering risks, and see themselves as pillars of a competitive but responsible private-enterprise system. Yet, when crises and panics occur, governments are expected to provide lender of last resort liquidity facilities, organize and pay for bail-outs of institutions deemed 'too big to fail', and ensure depositors are fully protected. Yet, over and over again, throughout history, there have been episodes of over-eager lending, reckless investing and poor risk management, leading to financial failure and calls for help. This current crisis is supposedly different because the securitization of debt gave the appearance of liquidity and sophisticated risk management. But it also had the same common themes of greed and stupidity. A system that allows banks and other institutions to make profits and fat salaries from questionable and foolish practices, while the public picks up the bill, should simply be unacceptable. The question is: what is the alternative? I return in a later chapter to the issue of how the financial system might be reformed so as to avoid, or reduce, these risks. But I turn now to a different aspect of the storm, the turbulence generated by oil prices.

3

The Latest, or Last, Oil Shock?

In June 2004 a Sunday newspaper ran a fantasy horror story: 'What If Bin Laden Conquers Saudi Arabia?' In this scenario, crude oil prices 'are nudging $100'. In the real world, bin Laden is still in his cave and the accommodating Saudi royals were until recently pumping as much oil as they could. Yet oil nonetheless touched $140 per barrel in mid-2008. Fact proved to be more dramatic than fiction. What happened? And why did it happen during a financial crisis already causing difficulties enough for the world economy? Prices have since more than halved from their peak and have fallen as low as $40 per barrel. Should we be more concerned about the boom, or the bust? The links between the recent oil shock and the financial crisis and global recession are indirect but very important, and in this chapter I try to trace them.

Oil has been part of the boom and bust cycle of economies before. Rapid economic expansion and contraction, and financial manias, have long had repercussions for commodities in general and oil in particular. In the Great Crash of the early 1930s, following an earlier boom, oil prices fell through the floor and one of the tasks of the Roosevelt's New Deal was to support them. Harold L. Ickes, Roosevelt's energy secretary, noted that oil companies 'were crawling to Washington on their hands and knees these days to beg the government to run their businesses for them'. Rather like banks today. He judged, as governments judge today, that 'there is no doubt about our absolute and complete dependence upon oil ... we have passed from the stone age to bronze to iron, to the industrial age and now to an age of oil'. (At the time US production was 66 per cent of the world total.) Ickes resolved to rescue the industry from the dire prospect of depressed prices. History may have come full circle since, barely three months after a panic about oil prices going through the roof, there is a growing panic about them falling through the floor, imperilling new investment. President Obama, like his predecessor, is being urged to understand the needs of the oil producers, albeit Arab as much as American.

Indeed, for most of its 150-year history, certainly since large supplies started to hit international markets from the US and the Caucasus in the 1880s, the preoccupation of the oil industry has been one of oversupply. Such concerns eventually led to the creation of OPEC. The two oil shocks of the 1970s and early 1980s radically changed the perception concerning 'oversupply' problems, but another decade and a half of weak prices reversed it again (with a brief interruption during the first Gulf War). The steady climb in oil prices this century to the heady heights of $140 per barrel in mid-2008 – with predictions of $200 (Goldman Sachs) and $250 (Gazprom) – has reopened once again the issue of whether we are in fundamentally new, uncharted waters or merely passing through another cyclical phase. A good case can be made for either position.

How did the recent oil shock occur? It crept up on us slowly in a way that the earlier shocks did not: the previous shocks (in 1973–4, 1979–80 and, arguably, 1990) were seen as being caused by specific, identifiable restrictions in supply. In fact, that is not true. These crises, like the present one, came at the end of a steady period of supply trying unsuccessfully to catch up with rising demand in the industrial and then the developing world. Supply disruptions merely highlighted how tight the margins of spare capacity were becoming. In the period after 1960–72, demand in the non-communist world more than doubled, from 19 million barrels/day to 44 million barrels/day (having more than doubled from 7 million barrels/day in 1945). The US accounted for just under 40 per cent of world demand, western Europe about one third, and Japan one tenth. The 'swinging sixties', in particular, were the era of unrestrained growth and booming oil consumption in the Western world and Japan: more, faster, heavier cars; rapid growth of oil consumption in power generation, plastics and petrochemicals. The USA, the world's largest oil producer, reached its highest-ever oil production peak of 11.3 million barrels/day in 1971 and became a major importer by 1973 (at 6 million barrels/day). The Middle East became the 'supplier of last resort'.

But, quietly, the new sources of expanding supply in the Middle East – which met two thirds of the increased demand – were slipping under the control of producer country governments, with an assertive Iran under the Shah, the Ba'ath-led revolution in Iraq, Gaddafi's seizure of power in Libya, and the rise of nationalist politicians in Venezuela. The OPEC grouping had been established in 1960, quite innocuously, and its potential only gradually began to be appreciated by producers. By the early 1970s growth in demand was outstripping supply. A long period of low prices had blunted investment in the industry. Spare capacity was 3 million barrels/day in 1970, but it had slipped to 1.5 million barrels/day in 1973, roughly 3 per cent of demand. By the autumn it had fallen to 1 per cent, 500,000 barrels/day, as Kuwait and Libya cut production. This extraordinarily tight margin created a very similar situation to that in 2008. There was already great alarm in some countries, with animated discussion of an 'energy crisis' in the USA and panic-buying in the summer of 1973 by US and Japanese importers. Our collective memories of a problem caused by this long, slow build-up of demand relative to supply have subsequently been largely obliterated by the more visually striking pictures of the Yom Kippur War, launched on 6 October 1973. The Arab OPEC countries sought to use the 'oil weapon' – in practice, an embargo against the USA and the Netherlands, and all-round production cuts – and withdrew 5 million barrels/day at the most severe point of the embargo (albeit with some quirky, non-conforming behaviour, notably from Saddam Hussein who tried to help consuming countries and attacked the cutbacks of Arab 'reactionaries' for driving Europe and Japan into the arms of the USA). The ensuing scramble for supplies drove up the crude price from $5.40 to over $17 per barrel within two months. But in reality the 'supply shock' of the embargo simply amplified the 'demand shock' of demand having outstripped supply.

The embargo was short-lived, but the impact was profound and its political and economic legacies are still with us. Great prestige accrued to those who had anticipated the problem, albeit for different reasons: E. F. Schumacher, who published the 'anti-growth' *Small Is Beautiful* in 1973 (he was a strong advocate of coal); and the Club of Rome, which had published *The Limits to Growth* in 1972, warning of resource depletion (and also of global warming). The practical consequences of the shock for the Western world were a big push for nuclear power, a revival of coal, which had been losing ground to oil, a new preoccupation with energy conservation and efficiency, and, where possible, new oil exploration and production, as in Alaska, Mexico and the North Sea. The oil shock provided the impetus to a powerful market adjustment, both for demand and supply, which was reinforced by the second oil shock which commenced with the cessation of Iranian production in December 1978 in the upheaval of the Iranian revolution, which drove up prices from $13 to $34 per barrel. A panic scramble for oil, including 'gas lines' in the USA, fed demand, creating a speculative 'spike'. The Iranian crisis dragged on through 1980 and the oil market was beginning to stabilize when Saddam Hussein attacked Iran in September, further disrupting supplies from the Gulf, removing 4 million barrels/day of production and briefly driving up prices to $42 per barrel.

The major consequence of these two closely consecutive oil shocks was a very powerful economic response which, within a few years, had turned the oil famine into feast, scarcity into glut.

That process of market adjustment is crucial to understanding the big divide in opinion, now, as to the way the future will evolve. The oil pessimists, the 'peak oil' theorists, are heirs to the tradition of the Club of Rome, which predicted that demand growth is inexorably and unsustainably outstripping supply. That world view appeared to be vindicated by the experience of the 1960s and the first two oil shocks, and again in mid-2008. Oil optimists point to the remarkably rapid market adjustment that took place in the 1980s as being indicative of how flexible are both supply and demand when given powerful price signals.

What is undoubtedly true is that world energy demand was, for a while, very firmly knocked on the head. Oil consumption in the non-communist world was cut from 52 million barrels/day in 1979 to 46 million barrels/day in 1983. This fall was partly a consequence of recession, the deepest since the Great Depression of the 1930s. But there was also a combination of energy conservation and fuel switching. Conservation came from measures such as efficiency standards in vehicles. By 1985, the USA was 25 per cent more fuel efficient than in 1973 (measured by energy consumption per unit of GDP), and Japan over 30 per cent more efficient. Further savings came from the comeback of coal, nuclear power and (starting in Japan) natural gas. One crucial change was the disappearance of oil from power generation, leaving transport as its last bastion.

There has been, overall, a remarkable increase in frugality in the world's use of oil over the last three decades. The gas-guzzling USA has halved its oil intensity (measured as tons of oil in relation to real GDP). So have Europe and Japan, from a lower starting point to an even lower level. China has made even more spectacular advances, mainly because of the movement away from the extraordinary inefficiency of the Stalinist heavy industry favoured in the 1950s and 1960s.

In parallel, there was a rapid growth in non-OPEC production. Higher prices made oil exploitation and production highly profitable for the first time in many years. The main stimulus to production was in the USA, especially in Alaska and, later, the Gulf of Mexico, and in Mexico itself and the North Sea, but oil companies went looking for oil and found it in commercial quantities in Malaysia, Gabon, Angola, Egypt, Oman and China. OPEC was as a consequence forced to make the difficult choice between holding back production to support the price and maximizing revenue for development, leading to growing tension between the richer, low-population members, which could exercise restraint, and the poorer, higher-population countries. As oil prices plummeted in the mid-1980s, the oil producers desperately cut back their production, to 17 million barrels/day in 1985 – barely half of production capacity – in order to support the price. Budget pressures then forced them to increase production, driving prices down further. These were OPEC's darkest hours. The decision of Saddam Hussein to invade Kuwait in 1990 had much to do with a growing sense of financial desperation and tension between OPEC countries.

The upshot is that OPEC, despite having the lion's share of world reserves and almost all the world's low-cost oil, has not increased production, of around 32 million barrels/day, in an expanding world market, since a third of a century ago, before the first oil shock. The entire increment in production now comes from outside the OPEC countries. Back in 1973, OPEC produced over half of all the world's crude oil, but now it produces barely one third (32 million barrels/day out of 84 million barrels/day, in 2007).

Oil optimists cite this experience of diversifying production as proof of the ability of the oil industry to respond positively to 'scarcity' and higher prices. They expect to see the trick repeated again in the future, with non-conventional oils in Canada, through deep-sea exploration, and in new zones such as the Arctic and countries in Africa, Asia, Latin America and the former USSR which have not been intensively explored. Pessimists worry that production is falling behind demand growth and has peaked in those countries willing to produce more, leaving a greater dependence on the OPEC countries. They believe, furthermore, that OPEC has an incentive not to produce more but to let scarcity drive up the price, increasing the value of oil kept in the ground.

This background is important in order to understand what has been happening in this century. Until the oil market crashed in the latter part of 2008, there had been a steady upward climb from the day in December 1998 when oil prices fell to $10 per barrel, following a decade of low prices that had left the industry worrying that oil was becoming, as in the 1950s and 1960s, just another superabundant primary commodity, like coffee – not worth prospecting for in a world where production costs in difficult offshore fields and other 'new-frontier' exploration areas could be as much as $30–40 per barrel. Oil prices then started moving discernibly upwards from just over $25 in mid-2003 and broke through to $40 in May 2004. Newspaper stories started to appear about 'the next great oil shock' (*Financial Times*, 17 May 2004) and 'world braced for oil shock' (*Observer*, 11 May 2004). Prices continued remorselessly upwards ever since until the crash at the end of 2008.

The simple and obvious explanation for this prolonged rise is that the world economy has been growing very strongly in this century, faster than ever previously recorded. Specifically, there has been remarkably rapid growth in China, with 8–10 per cent annual expansion (Chinese numbers are not totally reliable, but few dispute this broad order of magnitude and the visible transformation of the country that has resulted from it). India is growing rapidly from a lower base. This expansion has fed into energy demand as industrialization has advanced and living standards have risen. Quite understandably, Chinese and Indian families wish to turn their increased income into the higher quality of life most of us take for granted: greater mobility, deriving from the ownership of vehicles; improved public transport and aviation; and comfortable levels of domestic heating, for example. China currently has around 40 million motor vehicles, less than the USA in 1949 and less than one fifth of the current US level (which stands at 250 million). In the first seven years of this century China and India accounted for 50 per cent of the increase in the world's primary energy demand (approximately 45 per cent from China alone), and 35 per cent of the increase in oil demand. With the slowing down of the main Western economies in the last two years, a substantial majority of the incremental demand for oil is coming from these countries, especially China. In the years from 2005 to 2007 inclusive, world demand grew by approximately 1.5 million barrels/day on average, and of that 1.3 million barrels/day came from non-OECD countries, led by China.

World oil supply, while growing, did not keep pace. We shall explore later whether this was the consequence of a fundamental long-term problem or of a series of conjunctural factors: underinvestment following a period of low prices; the Iraq War, following a decade of sanctions, which left production at around 2.5 million barrels/day, less than half the estimated potential; violence in oil-producing regions of Nigeria, causing substantial underproduction; US sanctions which have inhibited Iranian production, and Iran's own willingness to cut production to make a political point; disruption of production in Venezuela; and production falls in Russia. Much as in the early 1970s, steadily expanding demand, outstripping supply, ate away at spare capacity (much of which is in Saudi Arabia). From over 5 per cent of production in 2002 spare capacity fell to 2.5 per cent in 2004, and then to just over 1 per cent (1 million barrels/day). Saudi Arabia has expressed an intention to increase production capacity through a large investment programme, though this will be slow to come through. Any system operating on such wafer-thin capacity margins was dangerously poised for an extreme price reaction, which is what we have seen, just as we did in 1973. Yet the spike of prices in 2008 has passed. At the time of writing, prices were sliding back towards $40 per barrel as increased production met falling demand due to the global recession. We already seem far removed from the prediction of a $200 'super-spike', as Goldman Sachs analyst Arjun Murti proposed recently, which was reflected in the option contracts on oil at $200 per barrel.

This volatility prompts a series of questions. First, how much of the recent 'spike' can be attributed to 'speculation' rather than underlying supply and demand factors? Second, while an oil price shock represents a huge shift in relative prices and a cross-border redistribution of wealth (from countries that are not oil consumers to net oil exporters), what difference does it actually make to the world economy and its prospects for growth? Third, is it realistic to expect a repetition of the strong response, both in supply and demand, that occurred in the 1980s, driving oil prices further back down. Or is there now something fundamentally different about the oil world, as 'peak oil' theorists claim, which makes it inevitable that from now on oil prices will remain high when a recovering world economy encounters falling world production.

As prices soared towards $140 per barrel, scapegoats had to be found. The idea emerged that responsibility did not lie primarily with consumers for consuming 'too much' relative to supply, or with producers for producing 'too little' relative to demand (though consumers are blamed in oil-producing countries and producers in oil-consuming countries). Rather, the fault lay with 'speculators'. Oil consumers and producers have agreed on the pernicious role of speculators, if little else. There were, at one time, a dozen bills in the US Congress designed to deal with these malign forces of darkness. European leaders have been equally imaginative in coming up with wheezes to punish them: taxes on speculators, closing down markets in which they operate, unleashing criminal prosecutors against them.

There is a purist view – which I don't hold – that says that competitive markets will always be efficient even if they are volatile, since the price simply reflects the information available to market participants. I have noted in earlier chapters – in relation to housing, for example – that it is possible to have highly inefficient markets if prices are largely based on expectations of future price changes, especially in long-life assets. There is a separate argument, from the same ideological stable and with the same practical consequences, that speculators are inherently stabilizing in their influence on markets since they (collectively) only make a profit if they correctly anticipate the trends and turning points in the markets. In other words, they sell appreciating assets before markets peak, pushing down the price when it is soaring, or buy before markets hit rock bottom, pushing up the price. In practice, however, there are many examples of destabilizing speculation in the panics and crashes experienced in financial and commodity markets.

Was the recent spike a product of such 'destabilizing' speculation? It is perfectly reasonable to argue that in certain circumstances those who speculate in a commodity – in this case oil – can destabilize markets in an inefficient way. There was an example during the oil shocks of the 1970s. Motorists queued in 'gas lines', as they were called in the USA, to keep their tanks topped up, believing that scarcity would become worse and that prices would rise further. The consequential increase in stock levels held in tanks increased demand, and pushed up the price even further. Much oil was also wasted by motorists queuing at the pumps with their engines running. There were also reports of oil companies, industrial users, utilities and distributors hoarding stocks, or buying beyond expected consumption, in anticipation of higher prices to come. It was estimated that, in 1979–80, speculative accumulation of inventories by companies and consumers added 3 million barrels/day of demand above consumption, a larger amount than the actual shortage of production that caused the crisis. When the inventories were sold off in the falling market that followed, or motorists ran on lower tanks when prices fell, the 'speculators' lost money, but their losses did not provoke a lament from those who had earlier denounced speculative greed.

What evidence is there that speculation has been a major factor at work in the oil shock that we have recently experienced? No hard evidence has been put forward that there was systematic hoarding by companies or individuals. Perhaps because there has been no major supply disruption, people have not hoarded.

Instead of increasing demand in response to price increases, which is the effect of speculative hoarding, oil users have generally curbed demand, helping markets to stabilize.

A more subtle argument relates to forward markets. Investors buy or sell agreements forward, for future delivery. If they believe oil prices will rise in six months' time, they will enter into agreements now to buy oil at the current – 'spot' – price, and then sell at a profit in six months' time. This activity naturally affects today's spot price for those buying and selling oil in the spot market – but not any long-term contractual price for real oil already agreed between suppliers and refineries. In the example I have given, investors will push up the price today, but push it down relative to what it would otherwise have been in six months' time (since in six months' time they are contracted to sell oil). Depending on whether the overall position of those trading in futures markets is a net purchase of long-term positions ('net long') or a net sale ('net short'), this will drive today's price up or down. There is no doubt that substantial movements in spot prices are achieved in this way, but it is difficult to see evidence that the market has been pushed by speculative activity systematically in one direction. If there were, it would be reflected in the accumulation of inventories, as commitments to buy now in order to sell later are realized.

Critics try to make a distinction between regular traders in the real oil market, who close their positions by acquiring or disposing of real oil when their futures market contract expires, and those who are simply interested in speculating in 'paper oil'. They point to the big increase in money invested in commodity funds whose managers, in turn, invest in futures markets on their clients' behalf. It is claimed by Senator Joe Lieberman in the USA that the amount of money invested in 'index funds', which track commodity prices, has risen from $13 billion to $260 billion in five years, and that much of that money is in oil, perhaps accounting for 80 per cent of the commodities price index. While this latter is a large sum, it is only one half of one per cent of oil market transactions in a year. And, for the reasons given, there is little evidence of hoarding of real oil. There have also been falling prices in other industries where there are active commodity markets (such as nickel), and rising prices where there are not (such as rice). Attempts to blame high oil prices on financial speculators therefore seem wide of the mark, even though they contribute to short-term volatility. Perhaps the need for a scapegoat stems from the sense of impotence in seemingly powerful countries like the USA and Germany, which feel that they are essentially passive price takers in a market dominated by China on the demand side and Gulf Arab (OPEC) states on the supply side.

This is not to say that oil markets are in any sense normal or working well. Prices should approximate to the cost of producing an extra unit – the long-run marginal cost, variously estimated at $10–60 or $70 per barrel, depending on where the extra unit is ($10 in Iraq or Saudi Arabia, $60 or $70 in the Arctic or Canadian tar sands). The world price rose a lot higher than even the highest estimate of marginal cost. There was, in that broad sense, a speculative 'bubble'. The difference – the 'rent' in the language of economists – was accruing to producer countries that were not allowing these extra units to be produced. This could be seen as a calculated and speculative punt by the producers on the fact that future oil would be worth a lot more than present oil. If so, they badly miscalculated, because the price has since slumped to a level well below that which almost all producing countries regard as the minimum necessary for their domestic requirements.

If there were clear evidence that speculative behaviour in futures markets was badly and systematically distorting the price in an upward direction, governments could counter it by releasing government-held strategic stocks so as temporarily to flood the market and punish the speculators. The US stock alone is 680 million barrels, the equivalent of 4 million barrels/day for almost eighteen months. So far, the judgement has been made that there is no justification for using this stock as a buffer to counter market trends rather than as a strategic stock to counter a possible embargo. The judgement has been vindicated by the fact that the market fell sharply without any intervention.

———————

The increase in oil prices to $140 per barrel was a major ingredient in the witches' brew of economic toxins that contributed to the crisis of 2008. First, a big increase in oil prices operates like an indirect tax on the world economy. It is simultaneously inflationary – it pushes up prices – and deflationary – it reduces consumer purchasing power. Much then depends on how major consuming countries react to this mixture of inflation and deflation. During the 1978 shock the leading governments and central banks were preoccupied with virulent inflation and the dangers of a wage–price spiral and sharply increased interest rates – at one point the US prime rate reached 21.5 per cent. There was a recession, and this recession was transmitted to the developing world via falling commodity prices and the impact of high interest rates on their debt. On this occasion, oil-consuming countries have engineered both recession and inflation, but the emphasis has shifted to fighting recession via interest rate cuts. That, however, is not the end of the story. The OPEC countries act like a tax-gathering government and spend their revenue. During the first and second oil shocks this process provided an initially slow but growing offset to the forces of recession, and it is doing so again.

The OPEC countries, moreover, do not require oil-importing countries to send them goods and services to balance their transactions. They accept future claims in the form of financial securities, property or other investments. This process – 'recycling' – was the subject of much agonizing and analysis in the late 1970s, but now it simply happens. To work, it requires a degree of trust by the oil exporters that their investments will be safe and remunerative, and a willingness by oil-importing countries to accept OPEC claims – be they rich foreigners buying expensive property and football clubs, or companies (or banks) being taken over, in whole or part, by sovereign wealth funds.

The efficiency of recycling has been one factor blunting the economic impact of an oil shock on oil-consuming countries. Another is that in the three and a half decades since the oil shocks of the 1970s Western economies have become much less oil-dependent. Deindustrialization, switching fuels and energy conservation have all played a part in reducing the amount of oil consumed as a proportion of GDP by over 50 per cent. It is possible to deduce from the oil intensity of the economy the first-round impact on prices (that is, excluding the effect of taxation and any second-round effects of interest rates and other policies). Roughly speaking, and based on exchange rates in mid 2008, a $10 per barrel increase over a year raises inflation by 0.2 per cent in the UK, 0.25 per cent in the eurozone, and 0.4 per cent in the USA. Since there was virtually a $100 per barrel increase in price after 2003–4, there was a – one-off and gradual – inflationary shock of 2 per cent in the UK, 2.5 per cent in the eurozone, and 4 per cent in the USA. But those impacts pale into insignificance beside those in developing countries, which have in the process of development become much more energy-dependent. On the same measure, a $10 per barrel oil price increase raises inflation by around three times the OECD average in India, and well over twice in China and Africa as a whole. This helps to explain why most developing countries have been struggling to keep inflation within single figures. They have also had to face food inflation, which is highly sensitive in poor countries, accounting for 30–60 per cent of family spending. The significance of this 'double whammy' from food and energy, I pursue below.

Overall, however, the factors that dragged down the world economy a third of a century ago have been less in evidence. Indeed, the world economy continued to grow strongly up to and including 2007, despite the steady increase in oil prices. One major reason was the ease with which the banking system, until its collapse, acted as a financial intermediary, transferring the surpluses of oil exporters back into the economies of oil-importing countries. Goldman Sachs has estimated that $1.8 trillion was being transferred from oil consumers to oil producers in 2008. The oil producers saved in aggregate around half of their windfall and spent the rest. The $1 trillion a year of excess savings was being accommodated by the oil-importing world in the form of capital inflows. The capital inflows financed large current account deficits in some oil-importing developed countries (the USA, UK, Spain, Poland) and emerging economies (South Africa, Pakistan, Turkey). Despite the efficiency of this financial recycling, the oil shock none the less added an extra destabilizing load to an already unbalanced world economy.

———

As I have described above, the world was able to cope with the oil shocks of the 1970s by recycling oil producers' surpluses in the short run, and in the longer term by a process of adjustment through the response of demand and supply to price signals. The evidence from the past suggests that both demand and supply do respond, given time. Some modelling by Nobel laureate Gary Becker at the University of Chicago suggests that in the developed world oil consumption drops by only 2 to 9 per cent in response to a doubling of oil prices, within a space of five years; but over longer time periods consumption drops by 60 per cent. On the same assumptions, supply grows by only 4 per cent within five years, but by 35 per cent in the longer term. The story behind these figures is not difficult to put together. In the short term, consumption may not respond quickly to higher prices (unless there is also a fall in income and purchasing power). It takes time for individuals to change their make of car, for manufacturers to produce new, fuel-efficient, cars, for people to move so as to reduce their dependence on car commuting, for electricity generators to change their feedstock, or for new materials to appear that are not oil-based. But once these adjustments are made, their effects can be far-reaching.

It is now the response of the developing, rather than the developed, countries that matters, much more than in the 1970s. One major factor slowing response in the short run – but not the long run – is the existence of government subsidies for oil products (or a reluctance to tax them as much as in some rich countries). China has lower petrol prices (around 75 cents per litre) than the USA ($1 per litre), and a third to a half of those in Britain or Germany. It may be understandable why oil-rich Saudi Arabia or Venezuela should decide to make petrol available to their people for a few cents a litre. But Indonesia, Mexico and Malaysia have many other claims on public resources, and oil subsidies are unaffordable (at 7 per cent of GDP in Malaysia, and 3 per cent in Indonesia, before recent price increases). India's oil subsidies have been running at around 2 per cent of GDP, a major contributor to an unsustainable budget deficit (9 per cent of GDP and rising). Governments are naturally reluctant to take on protesting objectors, but few doubt that they will have to, and are already doing so.

It is the supply response that is more controversial. World oil production grew, over thirty years, from 55 million barrels/day in 1983 to 80 million barrels/day in 2007, an increase of roughly 1 million barrels/day each year. If demand growth continues at present trends, production will have to grow to 140 million barrels/day by 2030 to keep prices broadly stable. There are wildly divergent views as to whether this is a feasible objective (even if it were desirable).

————

There are basically two theories about the future of oil. One is the theory of 'super cycles'. On this view, we shall lurch from current scarcity and high prices to superabundance and low prices, and then back again, as has occurred over the last few decades. Cycles operate as they do in – and may be correlated with – financial markets. The other is 'peak oil' theory, that we have finally reached the limits of production: that it is downhill all the way for production (and uphill all the way for prices). The outcome of this controversy is crucial for the world economy. There are ideological overtones – 'greens' versus 'brown' oil interests – and psychological ones too – pessimists versus optimists. But the key difference is over a set of facts, as interpreted by geologists and economists.

'Peak oil' theory has recently enjoyed considerable prestige and a strongly sympathetic, fashionable literature, though the collapse in prices in late 2008 is an inconvenient twist in the story. In one, obvious, logical sense, 'peak oil' theory must be right: oil is a finite resource and production must peak at some point. But the 'peak oil' theorists say that that point is now, or at least imminent. Even if new oil is discovered, they argue, it can do no more than offset the falling output of known fields. There is no prospect, they maintain, of substantially raising production on the scale required by current demand growth and as confidently predicted by the International Economic Association, the official intergovernmental voice of oil-consuming countries (and 'optimists'), which bases its judgements in significant part on the US Geological Survey.

The 'peak oil' argument, considerably oversimplified, is this: there is a history of peaking in established, known fields. Most famously, M. King Hubbert was a Shell geologist who correctly predicted in the mid-1950s, in the face of some scepticism, that US oil production would peak around 1970 and then decline. It did (though Alaska emerged subsequently, and there have been recent major discoveries deep offshore in the Gulf of Mexico, albeit with offshore drilling constrained by environmental legislation). The North Sea has passed through the same peaking process – indeed, it peaked ten years later than 'peak oil' forecasts claimed it would – and it is estimated that eighteen individual countries, accounting for around 30 per cent of production, have passed their peak.

There has been evidence, carefully evaluated by Matthew

Simmonds, that the big fields in Saudi Arabia, notably Ghawar, the world's largest field, which produces 5 million barrels/day, have serious depletion problems, reflected in high water content in major wells. The Saudis are very secretive, but Simmonds has concluded that production is being maintained only with difficulty and has peaked. Kuwait has also been found to have exaggerated its reserves.

Furthermore, the oil companies are an important source of estimates of resources, but, 'peak oil' theorists argue, have an incentive to boost the figures to the maximum in order to inflate their share price. Shell was caught in the act in 2004, creating a major scandal at the time, and there is a continuing debate as to whether this was a one-off event or a systematic distortion. There is also an opposite argument, advanced by Richard Pike of the Royal Society of Chemistry, that companies tend to *underestimate* resources so as to inflate the oil price and hence their share price. The big technological 'fixes' that have lifted the oil industry in the past may raise production, but they do not produce more recoverable oil, so the wells deplete that much the faster.

To this set of points, there is an equally formidable reply – though, since it mainly comes from people described as 'insiders' in the oil industry, it does not have the same ring of publishable authority, with a few exceptions such as Peter Odell. He claims that conventional oil will not peak until mid-century, and unconventional sources such as Canadian tar sands not until the end of the century. Morris Adelmen of MIT has argued that 'the amount of oil available to the market over the next 25 to 30 years is for all intents and purposes infinite'. This optimism is based on several considerations.

First, proven reserves are reported as having increased by 1.5 billion barrels over the last three and a half decades (though just over half that amount has actually been consumed), so that predicted years of supply are increasing, not decreasing. Some of this increase in reserves represents new discoveries, but much of it represents revisions in the light of technological advances and higher prices (reservoirs have increased their recovery rate from 20 per cent to 35 per cent over that period). Critics say that oil companies exaggerate, that the big numbers hide gradations of confidence, and that rising reserves may well coexist with declining production. Nevertheless, the fact is that oil reserves are rising despite unprecedented economic growth

Secondly, many parts of the world are largely unexplored. India recently produced a substantial field onshore in Rajasthan and claims that there may be big undiscovered fields offshore. Brazil has identified a large offshore field, and the South American Atlantic continental shelf is mostly unexplored, as is Africa's, albeit with several fields already identified and producing in Nigeria, Angola, Equatorial Guinea and elsewhere. Russia has not been explored with the latest technologies. There are reportedly numerous potential fields in Iraq (which, even without invoking conspiracy theories, is undoubtedly one of the reasons for the US presence there). The Saudis argue that there is enormous unexplored potential in the Iraq border area. The list is long, even without invoking exotic possibilities like the North Pole (a recent survey by US geologists has suggested that the Arctic may contain a fifth of the world's undiscovered but recoverable resources, amounting to 90 billion barrels of oil, enough to supply the world for three years, most of it in Arctic Alaska). It can be argued that depressed prices over two decades explain the underinvestment in developing this potential. Between 1998 and 2008 spending on exploration by the top ten oil companies fell from $11.3 billion to $8 billion.

Thirdly, low prices, have caused research and development to be cut back. But enough technology is known and developed for the companies to be able to say that much more can be extracted from existing fields, as well as new ones, using steam injection techniques, 4-D seismic analysis, or electromagnetic detectors. And it is now possible to drill deeper underground and underwater. Development wells are no longer hit and miss but almost 100 per cent accurate.

Then, there is the brave new world of non-conventional oils, now at last beginning to be developed in Canada, which can potentially multiply reserves many times over. There are some formidable obstacles, not least a highly polluting extraction technology, the destruction of forests and high costs. But the problem is not geology or chemistry. The oil industry has long argued that non-conventionals will fill the gap left by conventional oil, just as what is now called conventional oil filled the gap created by the last 'peak oil' problem, when the sperm whale was hunted to near-extinction in pursuit of its blubber in the mid-nineteenth century.

These are finely balanced arguments, and my own economist's leanings are with the optimists. It may be, however, that 'peak oil' theory is right for the wrong reason: politics rather than geology. No amount of technology will boost exploration or production if producing countries are unwilling or unable to utilize it. Several major producers are hobbled by conflict or political instability – Iraq, Iran, Nigeria and Venezuela – while Saudi Arabia's political stability cannot be guaranteed. Even where there is stability, resource nationalism is potent. Nationalized industries dominate in almost every major producing country outside the Anglo-Saxon world, even in developed countries like Norway. There are moves to close off access to private, especially Western, oil companies in Russia. And other non-OPEC producers – Brazil, India, China, Mexico, Malaysia – give a dominant role to state-owned or state-dominated companies even at the expense of access to capital and technology, at least in the short term. Government-owned companies now control about 73 per cent of world oil reserves, 55 per cent of gas reserves, and half of all oil and gas production. It may be that these companies will mimic multilateral oil companies – as some already are doing – by investing overseas, raising capital in international markets, welcoming minority investors and collaborating over technology. But there is also a fear that corruption, incompetence and politicization will undermine the capacity to explore and produce.

Two other factors may inhibit the growth in production necessary to break free from 'peak oil'. The economics of collective monopoly, or cartel, behaviour do not suggest that it is in the interests of producers to maximize production. Particularly the rich and less populous OPEC countries have every incentive to keep oil in the ground if they calculate that the resulting appreciation in price will exceed the return they can obtain by producing, exporting and holding income-yielding securities. Another is that most oil-producing countries have had experience of the negative effects of oil: the so-called 'curse of oil'. Oil brings riches, but it can also bring massive waste, corruption, unsustainable spending and over-concentration of power. Overvalued exchange rates make manufacturing and agriculture uncompetitive. Smarter governments now channel much of their oil income into 'stabilization funds', distributing the proceeds slowly. Others simply do not produce as much. Peak production may not be a function of geology as much as of these political and policy constraints. The practical implication is that when the world economy recovers from the current slump in growth, and oil demand, it may hit up against oil supply constraints quite quickly, and we may find that the main oil producers are not at all accommodating.

The discussion so far has been conducted on the assumption that the energy price shock has been exclusively about oil. Actually, world demand for primary energy is, very roughly, equally divided between coal, oil and gas (with non-fossil fuels having about 20 per cent). The other primary fuels have also been subject to the same demand factors pulling up prices. Coal may present environmental problems, but not the concerns about peak supplies and restriction of supply that apply to oil; only a relatively small proportion of coal that is used is internationally traded; supplies are vast relative to current demand; and the big exporters, notably Australia, have no inhibitions about supplying the market. If the 'peak-oil' theorists are right that we are heading for tight oil supply and high prices, one consequence may be an environmentally unfriendly switch to coal as well as dirty non-conventional oils. Gas supply is potentially more problematic.

Until recently, gas attracted little attention. It was seen as essentially worthless or, at best, a side product from oil development. To this day, large volumes of gas are flared off, rather than used productively, most controversially in Nigeria. But the attractions of gas as a relatively clean fuel have grown, since it produces less pollution than coal and less carbon per molecule than oil or coal. Other than piped gas for domestic heating, gas has substantially displaced coal for power generation in the UK, Germany, Japan and the USA. It is also being turned into liquids with potential as a transport fuel. Unlike oil, however, gas is not easily transported without large infrastructure and logistics investment, which meant that, until recently, markets were essentially regional rather than global. Transporting gas to remote markets requires compressing and cooling it and shipping it as natural gas. It is only within the last few years that LNG 'trains' (that is to say, ships) have been developed to supply significant gas importers like Japan, the UK, the USA, India and China.

What has promoted gas from the footnotes to the main text is the fact that one quarter of world reserves, and just under a quarter of production, originates in Russia and is controlled by its majority state-owned gas company, Gazprom. Russia is the dominant supplier of gas to eastern and western Europe, through big pipelines across Belarus and Poland, with another through Ukraine and the former Czechoslovakia. Germany now takes 30 per cent of its gas from Russia; France and Italy are major customers; and the UK may become so after around 2015. Although the USSR proved to be a reliable supplier of gas during the Cold War years, the worry has begun to grow either that Russia will seek to exploit a dominant supplier position to extract higher prices or that politics will intrude, with gas becoming a 'strategic' weapon. The cutting off of supplies to Ukraine and Georgia for what appeared to be political reasons has fuelled this anxiety.

Such concerns have undoubtedly played a role in persuading the British government to support new nuclear power. A calmer analysis would suggest that these fears are greatly exaggerated. It is possible to secure a wide diversity of gas supplies (for the foreseeable future, Britain's supplies will be from the British, Dutch and Norwegian North Sea, and increasingly from LNG). There is a severe dearth of the storage capacity that would, if built, enable the economy better to withstand shocks – as is already the case in Germany, Italy and France. Gas price surges – which took prices from under 40p per therm in January 2007 to 100p per therm in mid-2008 – have much more to do with the poorly functioning EU market than the global market, or Russia. Russian (and other) gas exporters have as much interest in security of demand as importers have in security of supply. The separate – and almost certainly exaggerated – fears about gas supply nonetheless amplify the political disquiet about energy supply.

The collapse of oil prices in the latter part of 2008 has, for the moment, removed worries about the impact of an oil price shock on consuming countries. It is possible that, as in the 1980s, the issue will recede into the background, allowing the world economy to recover from the financial storm and recession. But that is optimistic. There remains the capacity for further serious disruption if production fails to expand. Indeed, the collapse of oil prices makes that more likely than not. Some OPEC countries could be plunged into political instability, which would disrupt production. State oil companies will have their coffers raided in order to keep their governments' budgets afloat. The oil multinationals will cancel investment projects that are no longer viable. When the world economy next recovers, there may not be the capacity to respond.

If the pessimists about future high oil prices are correct, for the right or the wrong reasons, the risk of future oil shocks may, however, be an opportunity as much as a threat. High prices for oil and other fossil fuels will stimulate both the development of renewables and investment in energy-efficiency in a way that no amount of moralizing and hectoring by governments has been able to do. The high price of oil is a form of carbon tax which governments, on their own, would be terrified of imposing on their citizens but are privately relieved to see oil markets do on their behalf, thus helping to curb carbon emissions. To achieve a benign outcome, increases in price, and the necessary adjustment to them, have to occur gradually and predictably without sudden disruption and extreme spikes. If these do occur, then there will be panic populist measures, such as price controls and subsidies. There may also be a scramble for secure supplies and the use of bilateral agreements or military threats in order to obtain supplies on favourable terms. Were this to happen, much damage would be done to the world economy, involving not just oil production but, potentially, the financial flows associated with it. Therein lies the challenge to policy makers: to maintain, through both national and international measures, a stable long-term framework that can survive the inevitable fluctuations in prices. Producer and consumer governments should be discussing a target range for prices and how stock management can support it. If that proves politically or technically too difficult, the oil shocks of 2008 will return in an even more extreme and violent form.

4

The Resurrection of Malthus

The energy price shock, combined with a banking crisis and bursting property market bubble, has been challenging enough. The oil price shock, however, coincided with, and was part of, a wider surge in commodity prices, including food. A big increase in oil prices has had major implications for those whose lives depend on the cost of transport and other fuels. But food is even more basic. If people cannot afford it, they starve.

Like oil prices, food prices have long experienced cyclical spikes. Indeed, these go back through the mists of time since agriculture became commercialized. But within the period of statistically recorded economic history, there have been very sharp increases in basic grain (wheat) prices in identifiable major markets, which saw extreme peaks during the Napoleonic Wars (a more than doubling of prices from those of the mid-eighteenth century) and in the 1840s and mid-1850s; then, preceded by lesser peaks, a tripling of prices after the First World War; a further tripling from a pre-Second World War low to the Korean War peak; and again in the 1970s. There are strong historical parallels between the simultaneous food and oil price shocks of the 1973–4 period and those of recent years: the same steady decline in stocks (or spare capacity) in a world of steadily rising demand, leading to an explosive surge in prices.

Just as there are parallels in the cyclical extremes of the market, there are parallels too in the way a crisis environment has changed our way of thinking about food and raw materials. The 1970s popularized the Club of Rome's *Limits to Growth*, while the current crisis has created a new orthodoxy around 'peak oil' and, in the case of food, has brought about a revival of the ideas associated with Thomas Malthus. His work first appeared at the turn of the nineteenth century, before the industrial revolution was fully under way. He was preoccupied with the problem of what he saw as inexorable population growth hitting up against finite supplies of food, restricted in supply by finite fertile land, resulting in the 'positive check' of famine, disease and war. Malthus has long been dismissed as a false prophet who failed to anticipate the 'demographic transition' to lower birth rates and the capacity of human ingenuity and technology to increase food supplies and patterns of trade to distribute them. But, while no one would seriously try to reinstate Malthusian pessimism in its pure and original form, its central idea of 'limits to growth' has acted as a counterpoint to the inexhaustible optimism about the potential of technology and economic dynamism that surfaces in long booms. The ideas of Malthus were taken forward by John Stuart Mill (who, in a prescient understanding of today's world, was also the first economic thinker to produce a coherent explanation of boom and bust cycles in financial markets). And there is now, in that tradition, a well-developed 'neo-Malthusian' world view, which is highly influential in today's debates.

While the oil shock emerged gradually, and began to be anticipated by many commentators in 2003–4, the sharp increase in food prices was much more sudden. Between April 2007 and April 2008 maize prices in world markets increased by over 50 per cent, wheat and vegetable oil prices doubled, and rice prices almost trebled. At the beginning of August 2008, food prices overall were 150 per cent higher than in the same period in 2000, and 40 per cent up over the previous year. These price changes are broadly comparable to those for industrial raw materials, though less dramatic than for oil and other energy prices. There was also a big shift in relative prices as against manufacturing. Just as oceans of ink were spilt in the 1950s and 1960s explaining the inexorable decline of commodity prices relative to those of manufactured goods, and again in the 1980s and 1990s, the inky currents were now swirling in the opposite direction.

On the demand side, the rapid growth of the world economy fed through into food markets as well as other consumables. It is surely a matter for rejoicing that after millennia of subsistence on a bowl of rice a day, hundreds of millions of Asians now enjoy a more varied diet. China alone accounts for up to 40 per cent of the increase in global consumption of soya beans and meat over the past decade, while the pigs, cows and chickens that provide this meat also consume grain as part of their diet. In India, where levels of nutrition are still lower than in China, though growing, and meat is less desired for cultural reasons, increased domestic demand has led to increased imports (or reduced exports) of vegetable oils, grain and sugar. The IMF *World Economic Outlook for 2008* concluded that China, India, Brazil and Russia together accounted for 80 per cent of the rise in demand for grains over the last five years.

Another component of demand has been a switch from food grains to biofuels to counter the energy crisis and reduce carbon emissions. Biofuels based on vegetable oils or grain inevitably diminish food for human consumption, either directly or indirectly by encouraging changes in the pattern of land use away from foodstuffs. The IMF has estimated that while biofuels account for only 1.5 per cent of liquid fuel supplies, they accounted for half of the increase in consumption of major food crops in 2006–7, mainly because of corn-based ethanol production in the USA. The World Bank has reported that the USA has used 20 per cent of its maize for biofuels, and the EU around 70 per cent of its vegetable oils. Much of this biofuel is subsidized, either directly or though protected, guaranteed markets.

On the supply side, the most important, and worrying, trend – and the one seized upon by the neo-Malthusians – is the slowing productivity growth of the main food crops in developing countries. The green revolution of the 1960s, when hybrid crops first boosted yields of rice and wheat, was followed in the 1970s by a big increase in output following a surge in the price of foodstuffs. But yields are unmistakably falling. Maize yields grew on average by around 3 per cent per annum in the 1960s and 1970s, but are now growing at just over 1 per cent. Wheat had explosive, double-digit percentage yield growth in the early 1960s, which settled down to around 4 per cent growth for a couple of decades, but has since fallen to under 2 per cent. Rice yield growth has fluctuated to give an indistinct trend, but appears to have fallen from 2–4 per cent in the three decades since the start of the green revolution to about 1 per cent.

These yield growth falls matter because one of the consequences of increased population in many of the most populous developing countries is that there is little unused land left for cultivation – or it can be cultivated only by eating into valuable environmental resources such as forests. There are vigorous debates as to why the green revolution has run out of steam, though Malthus, and his contemporary David Ricardo, would have made the simple point that there are diminishing returns to the application of more and more fertilizers, insecticides and other 'scientific' inputs. In practice, water supply has been a key limiting factor, preventing the spread of technologies that depend on irrigation. There has been much less success in raising yields in rain-fed agriculture, which is the norm in most of Africa and in many parts of the Indian subcontinent. These countries also house the world's poorest people, who would lack the resources to invest in improved technology even if it were available to them.

This combination of supply and demand factors fed through into stock depletion. The total world stock of major crops, according to the IMF, halved from a peak of around 120 days in 2000 to sixty days in 2008. As stocks approached worryingly low levels, a scramble for supplies and market perceptions of impending shortages drove up the price, very much as occurred in 1973–4 and in previous food crises. One factor aggravating the crisis was the febrile behaviour of governments as well as markets. Exporters, such as Argentina, imposed export quotas to try to hold down domestic prices, and in the process aggravated the scarcity in international markets. Countries that traditionally maintained high levels of protection of their domestic farmers suddenly opened up to imports in order to meet domestic shortages, adding to demand for internationally traded foodstuffs and reducing incentives to domestic producers.

————

In developed countries higher food prices added to inflation, complicating the task of fighting incipient recession. The economic and social consequences of the food price shock, however, have been proportionately much greater in poor countries than in rich ones, since poor people spend a higher proportion of their income on food. It is estimated that while 10 per cent of family income is spent on food in the USA, the figure rises to 30 per cent for China, 50 per cent in Kenya and sub-Saharan countries at a similar level of development, and 65 per cent in Bangladesh. Yet the distributional effects of high prices are not straightforward. Countries that are net exporters experience a trade balance benefit in the form of increased (net) income for their producers; net importers experience the opposite effect. Exporters deriving a net benefit include Argentina, Brazil, much of the former Soviet Union, Indonesia, Malaysia and Thailand, as well as some developed countries such as the USA, Canada, Australia and France. Most of sub-Saharan Africa, the Middle East, China, the Indian subcontinent and Europe are net importers, with Africa taking a particularly big hit in terms of the trade balance. But there is also a complex balance of gain and loss within countries. Urban dwellers are hit by rising food prices, as are many landless rural labourers who have to buy food to survive. Farmers' gains depend on whether they can produce sufficient surplus to bring to market, whether they can market it at remunerative prices, and the balance of advantage between the foodstuffs (or crops) they produce and those that they consume.

The most visible sign of the impact of the food price shock was political unrest in the form of food riots, as seen in Haiti and Bangladesh. In the Horn of Africa there was outright famine, because war and political turmoil disrupted production and distribution, adding to the unkind vagaries of nature and the lack of purchasing power caused by extreme impoverishment.

For the most part, however, the impact has been less visible: what has been called the 'silent tsunami' of deepening poverty and malnutrition. Governments, aid agencies and charities reported that even at the height of the crisis food was generally available, but at prices the poorest people could not afford. The consequence was that they cut 'discretionary' consumption, such as school fees and medicines, in order to eat; switched their diet to cheaper, usually less nutritious items; or simply ate less. The powerful, but often misunderstood, insight of the Nobel laureate Amartya Sen – that famine and hunger are not primarily caused by a shortage of food, but by a lack of income – was put to the test on a big scale.

While there are some parallels between the oil shock and the food shock, there are several big differences. The first and most obvious is that food is a renewable, not a depletable, raw material. That distinction has to be qualified, since poor soil management, such as overgrazing, can and does lead to depletion, usually temporary but sometimes permanent, such as is occurring in semi-arid zones. There are also problems of fish-stock management, where overfishing leads to the threat of extinction, a problem greatly exacerbated by the fact that ocean fish stocks are not nationally owned and require cooperative management. These qualifications apart, there is nothing comparable to the self-interest of oil producers in restraining production in order to maximize the long-term value of their resource. In addition, it does not usually require years of project preparation, assembly of staff and equipment, and exploratory effort in order to produce more food in response to higher prices. As long as seed is available, the next planting season will suffice. There was a lot of evidence in 2008 of increased planting and, already, of increased production in the main food surplus economies in response to high prices. World prices have, as a consequence, receded from their peak. Where animals are involved (such as cows and pigs) adjustment is necessarily slower for biological reasons. But market adjustment is happening.

Can we therefore relax, knowing that there is no OPEC for food and that food exporters in particular, and farmers in general, are responding to the price shock by producing more, driving down the price? There are two big reasons why such complacency is in no way justified. The first is that world food markets are massively distorted by import and export quotas, subsidies, support prices and other interventions, which are enormously costly and generally (though not always) working to keep food prices higher than they would otherwise be. It is subsidies to biofuels that, more than any other single factor, have precipitated the recent food price crisis. The EU Common Agricultural Policy has devoted vast resources to the protection of farmers' incomes in the least efficient way, by encouraging overproduction, and latterly by incentivizing them not to produce, while blocking market access to competitive producers from overseas – at the expense of both those producers and EU consumers. The superficial attraction to poor countries of having surplus food dumped on them has in practice usually proved illusory, because it has undermined local small farmers.

The indefensible behaviour of the European Union is well matched elsewhere by the extreme protectionism of Japan and the increasingly lavish subsidies given to American farmers by the US administration and Congress. One of the few positive by-products of the recent food price shock is that it created the conditions – high prices for farmers – that should make it easier to dismantle the panoply of protectionist controls surrounding farming in these countries (and others). In practice, and disastrously, the effect has been the opposite. New or stronger export controls have been introduced in China, India, Vietnam, Argentina and Egypt. Much more importantly, the USA, with the complicity of the EU, led by France, and encouraged by the inflexible attitude of negotiators from developing countries (notably India), made no attempt to rescue the Doha Round of trade negotiations. A once-in-a-generation opportunity to make world markets in food work better was missed. The price will be paid in food-price instability next time there is a recovery in global growth.

A more fundamental point is that mass hunger in poor countries cannot simply be left to the process of market adjustment. This is a matter of basic humanity and ethics. Aid agencies understand, from past errors, that the best way to counter starvation or severe malnutrition is not to shower the poor with food from elsewhere – though properly managed food aid has a role – but to provide cash for social protection programmes and food-for-work schemes. The World Food Programme and other agencies are struggling at present to raise sums that are trivial when compared with the subsidies given to farmers in rich countries. There is a need for help with long-term investment, especially in rain-fed, developing-country agriculture, with technology comparable to that of the green revolution (which may include genetic modification). But the problem of malnutrition is not an easy one to resolve. It reaches into healthcare and education, both in general and specifically in relation to diet and hygiene, and requires the provision of advice, credit and comprehensive schemes for distributing seeds and fertilizers to hundreds of millions of small peasant farmers in order to raise their productivity. If this knot of interconnected problems is not tackled successfully, Malthus will be able to claim some belated, posthumous vindication. And while the developed world wrestles with its banking crisis and recession, this bigger, deeper issue will not go away.

5

The Awkward Newcomers

The storm has blown up at the point at which economic boom turned to bust: boom witnessed in the surge in oil, food and other commodity prices; and bust in the credit crunch, the consequence of a collapse in financial markets and the global banking crisis, linked in turn to a bursting bubble in major residential property markets. I have emphasized that these changes reflect long-standing cyclical fluctuations which have now come together in a spectacularly powerful and damaging way. But cycles alone do not explain what has occurred without reference to major structural change in the world economy, and in particular the growth of China and other major emerging economies.

To simplify greatly a complex argument with many nuances, the rapid growth of these emerging economies, especially China, has been generating demand for raw materials and food – growing more rapidly than supply and pushing up prices. The dependence of these countries on export-led growth also supplied the world with cheap manufactures, creating a non-inflationary environment which made it possible for the USA, the UK and other Western countries to grow so rapidly, without triggering overt inflation, over the last decade. But it also led to a large accumulation of current account surpluses, and these translated into large foreign exchange reserves which, combined with the surpluses and reserves of the raw material exporters, created a vast pool of liquidity which has flowed back into Western economies. While cheap manufactures created the conditions for low inflation and low short-term interest rates, the vast accumulation of – mainly – Chinese foreign exchange earnings manifested itself in the purchase of US government bonds, keeping down long-term interest rates. This liquidity and cheap capital provided the fuel for a credit boom and the massive expansion of financial markets, and drove up asset prices, especially in housing, to unsustainable levels: hence, in due course, the crash, and the storm. It is not too far-fetched to say that the 'nice' era of non-inflationary growth in Western economies has been built, mainly, on Chinese labour, and that the sophisticated structures of modern financial capitalism have depended on the continued cooperation and stability provided by the Chinese Communist Party.

––––––––

This process of mutual accommodation has to continue if there is to be a successful completion of the historically essential task of peacefully integrating the major Asian economies into the global economic and political system. We know from the experience of Germany and Japan in the earlier part of the last century that smooth, peaceful outcomes are not inevitable. The starting point has to be an understanding and recognition that what is taking place is not a sudden eruption from the economic bowels of the earth but a long-dormant volcano (or volcanoes) coming to life. Although it appears unfamiliar, even threatening, it is normal that two countries, China and India, each of which accounts for 20 per cent of the world's population, should dominate the world economy. They used to do so. Angus Maddison, drawing on some remarkable scholarship by economic historians, has shown that, two centuries ago, China accounted for around 35 per cent of the world's population and almost 30 per cent of world GDP, and India for 20 per cent of the world's population and around 16 per cent of GDP. The USA, today's superpower, scarcely registered, with 1 per cent of the population and 2 per cent of GDP. France, Britain and Russia were, after China and India, the big economic powers of the day. Before the nineteenth century, the dominance of the Asian powers was even greater. According to Maddison, China and India accounted for around 80 per cent of world GDP over the first eighteen centuries of the last two millennia.

Economic historians have long been puzzled as to why China, with its long history of scientific invention and innovative, sophisticated agricultural technology – which supported a sevenfold increase in population between 1400 and 1950 with no overall fall in living standards – should not have responded more quickly to the opportunities presented by capitalism and industrialization. Self-imposed isolation and prolonged upheaval played a big part. The stagnation of India, with its history of caste hierarchy, foreign rule and discouragement of entrepreneurship, is more easily explained. Both countries consequently missed out on the first wave of growth through globalization, and their growth and share of world GDP in the nineteenth and early twentieth centuries shrank to approximately 12 per cent (China) and 7 per cent (India) by 1913, and then down to 6 per cent (China) and just over 4 per cent (India) in 1950.

What has happened since is a strong rebound in growth, particularly since the emergence of Deng Xiaoping in China after 1978, and the economic reforms in India attempted hesitantly after 1980 and more decisively after 1990 under the direction of Manmohan Singh. Since the onset of Chinese reforms, an estimated 200 million fewer Chinese live in absolute poverty. And over the same period, the proportion of Indians living in absolute poverty has fallen from 60 per cent to 42 per cent (from 456 million to 420 million, out of a much increased population). Rapid growth has made China the world's second-biggest economy and India the fourth (ahead of, respectively, Germany and the UK) in terms of GDP measured on a purchasing power parity basis. There is much semi-theological debate around the measurement of GDP, but the broad magnitude and direction of change seems plausible. With India growing in recent years at around 7 per cent per annum, China at 9–10 per cent per annum, and the Western world at 2–3 per cent per annum before the recession, it is likely that, barring some disaster or political explosion preventing a continuation of these trends, China will have a bigger economy than the USA well before 2040. By then India will have an economy the size of Germany, Britain and France combined – with Brazil, Mexico and Russia each also having an economy bigger than any European country.

There are those who derive some comfort from being members of relatively rich and predominantly (but decreasingly) white societies that have been able to look down with a mixture of pride and pity on those who are less materially fortunate. They fear that any fundamental change in the world order will be at their expense: that the global economy is a 'zero-sum game', in which new competitors subtract from the well-being of already developed countries. Just as the arrival of large, boisterous, upwardly mobile immigrant families in a prosperous neighbourhood creates a shudder of apprehension among the established residents, the arrival of (mainly Asian) nouveaux riches on the world stage is not universally welcomed. The political and economic implications of these defensive attitudes will be explained in the next chapter.

For the moment, suffice it to say that, so far at least, the main Western governments have been wise enough to recognize the opportunities presented by the emerging economies, and the dangers of trying to frustrate their aspiration to higher living standards. Although the presidency of George W. Bush has been widely derided on account of the war in Iraq, future historians may judge that through his strategic commitment to working constructively with China – like his father, and Richard Nixon – he made a more important, positive contribution. The potential engagement of 40 per cent of the world's population in India and China (over 80 per cent if we take emerging economies as a whole), as they become integrated into the world economy and their incomes catch up with those in rich countries, should be a source of celebration – and also of self-interest and opportunity as hundreds of millions of new consumers spend their incomes on goods and services from the rich world as well as from each other. But it would be naive to imagine that this process will be free of friction, painful adjustment and big distributional consequences. And most of these concerns centre on China, which, in this century, has contributed twice as much to global growth as India, Brazil and Russia combined.

So far much of the growth of China (and India) has been internally driven, based on the spread of technology, improved practices in agriculture, and the growth of manufactures and services to meet internal demand. Particularly in China, there has also been an opening up to trade (and some foreign investment), both for the purpose of achieving access to raw materials not available domestically and – more tentatively – for the intrinsic benefit of trade competition, specialization and access to new ideas. In sheer aggregate terms, this process has not yet advanced all that far: China accounts for around 10 per cent of world trade (as against 4 per cent in 2000) and India barely 1 per cent. But it is changes at the margin that drive markets. To make the same point more dramatically, if simplistically, China and India, by joining the world economy, have effectively doubled the global labour force. It will be a long time before peasant farmers in rural backwaters of Bihar or Sichuan join the world economy. But the virtually limitless potential for trade and outsourcing to tap into this labour force is, in itself, proving an influence on business decisions and on wage-bargaining and costs in relation to many activities in richer parts of the world.

The pattern of specialization that has emerged is pretty much as the textbooks would have predicted. Asian economies use an abundance of labour to produce for world markets manufactures and traded services with a high labour content, and conversely import raw materials and capital goods. The impact on the world economy has been to change relative prices: pushing manufacturing prices down and raw material prices up. The simple model explaining this process was first set out by John Stuart Mill in

1848 (though he was more concerned with food prices than with oil). Raphael Kaplinsky has argued that China turned the terms of trade against itself by about 25 per cent, a big gain to the rest of the world (though China more than made up the loss through higher volumes traded).

The impact of the big Asian economies on the world economy has been heightened by the fact that the fall in manufacturing prices and the increase in raw material prices did not occur simultaneously but consecutively. In the early part of the century, it began to be noticed that the prices of many manufactured goods and many traded services were falling: not just clothes and shoes, but many consumer goods and engineering products. The effect was sufficiently large to push down the rate of inflation to below target levels, permitting a reduction in interest rates. Rather prematurely, some commentators saw the end of inflation. The overall impact on Western economies was benign in the short run, increasing the rate at which they could grow without triggering inflation and increasing consumer purchasing power by reducing the cost of living. At the time, this fortuitous windfall was presented as the consequence of brilliant economic management on the part of Gordon Brown and his peers. Few anticipated that there would be a nasty sting in the tail in the form of increased oil and food prices as the law of diminishing returns kicked in. It has been asserted at various times that the impact of China and the other emerging economies has been 'disinflationary' and 'inflationary'. It has been both at different times.

What is less ambiguous is the impact of changes in relative prices on the distribution of income. Owners and producers of raw materials, energy, agricultural goods and high-technology products have benefited, and mobile capital has benefited from access to new markets and access to low cost labour. Workers in competing industries – and, arguably, workers more generally, especially but not solely the unskilled – have been hit. The opening up of the world economy has brought into play a vast new labour force, so the obvious predicted consequence is that the returns to capital will increase relative to the benefits to labour. It is the same phenomenon on a much larger – global – scale that Marx observed in the nineteenth century as the rural masses poured into the cities of England (his 'reserve army of the unemployed'), holding down wages to subsistence levels and financing capital accumulation. It is not necessary to follow his argument to its extreme logical conclusion to see that in recent years real wages in developed countries, faced with this competition from Asia, have tended to lag behind productivity growth, while corporate profits have appeared to rise as a share of developed country income. In practice, technology, saving labour and deepening the use of capital, may well have been a more important factor than trade with Asia, but the two have interacted. Thus the emerging economies help to explain the apparently high share of profits in the national income, the relatively slow growth of real wages, as well as the combination of high oil and food prices with falling manufacturing prices. If the impact were limited to a change in relative prices and their distributional consequences, that would be important enough. But it has also been accompanied by major imbalances that have contributed, indirectly, to the wider crisis within the Western world's financial system.

––––––––––

When historians look back on the current period what they will find most odd, and different both from previous historical experience and from the predictions of theory, is the massive flow of savings from relatively poor countries such as China into rich countries, particularly the USA. The current account deficit – which is the mirror image of the net inflow of foreign capital – in 2008 was estimated to be over $700 billion for the USA and around $100 billion for the UK ($165 billion for Spain). The biggest surplus countries (net exporters of capital) are emerging economies – China at around $400 billion, other east and south-east Asian countries combined at around $130 billion, and the oil exporters, as discussed in the last chapter, with around $500 billion combined. Some rich countries continue to perform the traditional capital exporting role (Germany, Japan, the Netherlands and Switzerland), but their combined surplus – around $650 billion – is less than the deficit of the USA. It is these savings flowing into the international financial markets, mainly into the USA, that have supported consumption-led growth but have also generated the bubble economy whose collapse we are currently grappling with.

It is paradoxical and counter-intuitive that relatively poor countries should be supplying savings to the rich. In the late nineteenth century, Britain exported capital to the rest of the world. It accommodated this by running a current account deficit. Simple common sense, as well as more-sophisticated theory, suggests why this was sensible. British investors earned a higher return than at home, and emerging economies – such as Argentina, Australia, Canada and the USA – were able to use the inward investment to finance their rapid development. Yet now we have a perverse situation where investors (or governments) in emerging economies invest in American government securities rather than in their own countries, while the world's economic superpower apparently cannot generate enough savings to finance its own investment. The explanations for this strange phenomenon are several and tend to vary according to whom the author is seeking to blame.

The simplest and most direct explanation is that American (and British) consumers, and also governments, have been happily living beyond their means, but have been able to get away with it because of the easy availability of credit financed by the banking system, the expansion of which has been made possible by access to savings overseas. American households ran a surplus financial balance (savings minus investment) of 5 per cent of GDP before the Reagan boom years of the 1980s, but this fell to a deficit of around 8 per cent of GDP in 2005–6. The share of gross personal savings fell from 7 per cent to 2.5 per cent of GDP in the same period. The federal government's financial balance fell from very little to a deficit of about 5 per cent of GDP in 1983, and has fluctuated around that level ever since. This slippage was financed from abroad, with large current account deficits (currently placed at around 5 per cent of GDP) and a steady decline from a net foreign asset position to one of net liabilities.

The other way of looking at the same problem is from the Asian end. China has followed in the tradition of high levels of thrift of other Asian emerging economies such as Japan, Korea and Taiwan. No doubt the austerity engendered under communism discouraged heavy spending, and, until recently, the lack of availability of consumer goods also played a role. Also the lack of social safety nets means that the Chinese save for education, retirement and healthcare. However, the real drive behind Chinese savings is not frugal households – household saving, at 10 per cent of GDP, is actually lower than in India – but Chinese state-owned companies, which pay out no dividends, and the Chinese government itself. Gross savings as a share of the Chinese economy have reached an extraordinary 50 per cent, so there is capital to export even with an equally extraordinary 40 per cent going into investment. In other words, Chinese savers have generated considerably more savings than the economy has been able to absorb productively, even with the enormous surge in investment in infrastructure and industry.

But seen from an Asian perspective (and also, coincidentally, from an orthodox monetarist point of view), it is the USA, and the US monetary authorities in particular, which are to blame for allowing the situation to get out of control. Keeping nominal – and real – interest rates down, which was the legacy of Alan Greenspan's fear of recession, encouraged rapid credit growth and a boom in housing markets. Inflation was hidden because Asian manufacturers were keeping down the prices of goods. In reality, inflation was appearing in asset markets, notably housing. What should have happened, according to the critics, is that as costs fell due to the impact of Chinese labour on world markets, the benefits should have been passed on by making prices fall, so increasing real incomes. Instead, the main central banks saw deflation as a threat, not an opportunity, and cut interest rates unnecessarily, keeping inflation going. Investors were prompted by low interest rates to pursue higher returns in new-fangled risky assets, leading eventually to the credit crunch.

On this view, the Chinese savers are both heroes and victims: plugging the hole in the US (and UK) savings deficits, and then being ripped off by poor returns. And as the excessive spending spilled out into world markets, creating a big US trade (and current account) deficit and driving the dollar down, the savings-surplus countries now face an invidious choice. They could allow their exchange rates to appreciate, making their exports uncompetitive, or they could peg their currencies to the dollar (as China did), which forces them to intervene in currency markets, piling up reserves and potentially creating inflationary pressure. A little reflection will suggest that the weak link in the Asian response is their defence of currency pegs. Why should it matter if their exports become somewhat less competitive?

Western, especially American, critics answer the question unsympathetically and blame China for pursuing a deliberately mercantilist policy of holding down its exchange rates – until recently, pegged to the dollar – to help promote exports. This the Chinese have done by buying up lots of US Treasury bonds, keeping interest rates low in the USA, fuelling debt-led consumption, and allowing Americans to buy lots of Chinese imports. This has been called a system of 'vendor finance'. In its extreme forms, this argument portrays the USA as a helpless junkie manipulated into dependence by its cunning oriental drug-pusher, taking its revenge for the Opium Wars inflicted on it by the West. Angry Congressmen have threatened to punish China for this manipulative dominance obtained through unfair use of the exchange rate.

A more sophisticated and less emotive version of this argument nonetheless places responsibility firmly on the Chinese and other countries with a 'savings glut', as Mr Bernanke has called it. The thrifty Chinese are, in fact, villains for not making good use of their savings by investing them productively at home or abroad (individual Chinese are not allowed to own foreign assets). This failure generates huge capital flows, drives down long-term interest rates and the cost of capital, and these low interest rates create 'bubbles' in property markets and excessive borrowing in open countries like the USA. The heroic Americans act as 'borrowers of last resort', running a current account that has protected the world from recession – until now, when the process has ground to a halt. But the bottom line is that the Asians are to blame. They haven't learned how to spend.

The Chinese could answer that they have studied the experience of Japan and Korea, which achieved considerable success, leading to high living standards, through the growth of export-led manufacturing, with 'competitive' exchange rates and a restrictive – often overtly protectionist – approach to imports. China has a more liberal approach to imports than Japan has ever had, but there is still a strong element of mercantilist thinking: exports good, imports bad. Lessons, too, were learned from the Asian financial crisis a decade ago, when Asian countries with large current account deficits, which then included Korea, were seriously punished by the financial markets when confidence was lost and governments found themselves facing painful conditionality from the IMF. But since China's reserves are now well in excess of annual imports it is clearly over-insuring against the risk of balance of payments problems.

The complaint about China's 'unfair' exchange rate is, however, wrong on a basic point of economics. What matters for the 'competitiveness' of exchange rates is not the nominal value, but the real effective value when relative rates of inflation and the exchange rates of trading partners are taken into account. Chinese inflation is difficult to measure but is undeniably more rapid than in the USA, causing a real appreciation against the dollar. And when the dollar has appreciated against other currencies, it has taken the Chinese currency with it; in the period 1994–2001, it is estimated that China experienced a real effective appreciation of 35 per cent. Yet exports boomed, including in those markets where China experienced a loss of competitiveness (80 per cent of Chinese exports go outside the USA).

The reasons why China has sought to maintain a currency peg with the USA are only partly to do with export-promoting, mercantilist thinking. China has, as a result of years of current account surpluses and flows of direct foreign investment from multinational companies, acquired vast foreign exchange reserves, estimated at $1.8 trillion – out of a world total of just $7 trillion – mostly in the form of dollar assets. A currency appreciation against the dollar would have the effect of inflicting a large capital loss on China. Thus the dependence of the USA on China is mutual: the economic equivalent of mutually assured destruction. Were the Chinese abruptly to change their exchange rate strategy, as some American politicians demand, not only would it suffer a capital loss on its reserves but it could perhaps precipitate a disorderly collapse in the value of the dollar, with unpredictable consequences. So, in practice, it has agreed to a gentle, gradual, managed appreciation. Until December 2008 there were grounds for believing that the problem would be quietly resolved in this way. But then, panicking in the face of a sudden slowdown in exports and economic growth, consequent upon the global recession, the Chinese authorities effected a devaluation – reigniting the whole incendiary issue of exchange rate policy.

There are other reasons why the problems around the exchange rate may not be easily managed. As China becomes fully integrated into the world economy it will experience the same loss of national control over its domestic economy that Western capitalist economies have experienced. In technical terms, it can control its exchange rate or its monetary policy, but not both. While the USA and UK have opted for control of monetary policy and let their exchange rates float, China is trying to do the opposite. What is happening is that foreign reserves build up as a result of the Chinese central bank buying dollars in order to keep the exchange rate down. These reserves then feed through into an expansion of domestic money supply, which pushes up inflation. Specifically, what happens is that as the central bank buys large quantities of dollars it has to pay in its own currency. It then tries to 'sterilize' the increase in money supply by issuing a lot of government securities which are then 'parked' with Chinese banks. As China becomes a capitalist economy no longer governed by commands, banks have to have an incentive to hold these assets: this comes in the form of higher interest rates. If sterilization is successful, inflation is curtailed but foreign exchange reserves pile up – in China's case to well beyond the level needed for any conceivable shock. As interest rates increase to counter inflation, capital is attracted into China – 'hot money' – which requires even greater intervention, creating even more liquidity, and pushing up inflation. China is still theoretically a communist country and has capital controls, backed up ultimately by firing squads. But these no longer deter flows of capital, which operate through many subtle financial mechanisms, including over- or under-invoicing of trade and foreign investment transactions. Exchange rates therefore become, as they are for Britain or the USA, not independent tools of policy, but dependent on wider monetary policy.

One of two things can now happen. The first is for the Chinese to abandon their current policy, let the exchange rate float, accept big losses on their reserves, and reassert control over domestic monetary policy and inflation. This is the fantasy outcome of their US critics. But these critics should perhaps be careful what they wish for, since the result might well be a serious slowing of the Chinese economy at a time when the rest of the world economy is already moving into recession. There is already concern that this may be happening. And a big sale of their dollar assets by the Chinese – and other big reserve holders fearing a dollar devaluation – would force down the dollar, perhaps in a disorderly way.

The other, more likely, alternative is an attempted continuation of the status quo: holding down the Chinese currency. The status quo, however, has been fuelling inflation and monetary instability in China. It is also increasing tensions with the USA, which may now be aggravated by the recession there and anxiety about jobs, and spill over into protectionism. There has already been openly expressed resentment of Chinese (and other foreign) countries trying to improve their returns on dollar assets by switching into the purchase of American companies.

Those with long memories will recall that in 1971 the first Bretton Woods system broke down when the Nixon administration imposed an import surcharge and forced a currency appreciation on its main trading partners, aimed particularly at Germany and Japan. The USA may be tempted to try something similar again. President Obama has made commitments to labour unions to act tough on trade matters. Nor is the problem limited to the USA. A recent Harris poll suggested that almost 50 per cent of Italians and a third of French and Germans think that, for a mixture of political and economic reasons, China is 'the greatest threat to stability'. China ranked far ahead of Iran and other more plausible candidates. Indeed, the European dimension is perhaps not receiving adequate attention. If the USA stabilizes its current account deficit and the major Asian economies maintain their dollar exchange rates, then the burden of adjustment will fall on an appreciating euro. The strains are being felt not least in the relatively inflexible eurozone countries, which are struggling already to adjust to imbalances within the eurozone, notably Italy and other countries in southern Europe. It is not a coincidence that the most stridently anti-Chinese, and protectionist, noises are coming from semi-Fascists in the Italian government as well as US Democratic Congressmen.

The focus on China has also deflected attention from the other major source of surplus savings, the Middle Eastern oil exporters and Russia. The Gulf States also peg their currencies to the dollar, with consequences similar to those in China – not least growing inflation as a consequence of, in effect, adopting US monetary policy. But they are also different from China in that foreign assets are often privately owned, and hidden. They differ, too, in that their economies depend upon oil exports, and the collapse in oil prices that we have seen in the latter part of 2008 may make their surplus savings short-lived.

It may have been convenient for a while to allow the USA, the UK and other developed countries to finance their economic growth from overseas savings. And it may have been convenient for China (and some other emerging economies) to sustain short-term growth based on exports (and inward direct investment) by exporting savings and running large current account surpluses. Both take credit for the boom, and both must take part of the blame for the slump that has followed. Moreover, such an arrangement is perverse and has been giving rise to growing tensions making it unsustainable.

The USA is already adjusting under pressure of recession with a falling current account deficit. China will have to adjust in parallel or there is a risk that the tensions could break out into trade warfare. In other words, the USA cannot diminish its excess spending unless China – and others – diminish their excess savings. To do so would not be some act of philanthropy towards the USA. It would simply be sensible. Indeed, it is positively wicked for the government of a poor country to insist so stubbornly on the necessity of continuing to lend money to a very rich country rather than spending the money at home. What is needed is for the Chinese communists to behave more like communists and spend Chinese savings on social goods like healthcare and pensions instead of insisting on the privatization of these services.

––––––––

The world resembles an *Alice in Wonderland* tea party in that everything is the opposite of what it should be. Poor countries provide foreign aid to rich countries to help them live a riotous lifestyle. Rich countries then become angry that they are being forced to accept aid from poor countries and argue that this state of affairs is desperately unfair – not to the poor countries, but to themselves. Poor countries complain, in turn, about being bullied into stopping this flow of foreign aid from their own people who need it to foreigners who don't.

But this world is positively rational compared to the mad, mad world of trade policy. The main trading countries have been locked for several years in negotiations that centre on the following proposition: you agree to stop shooting yourself in the foot by paying out subsidies and hurting your consumers through costly import restrictions, and we shall, reluctantly, do the same. Or, more accurately, if you refuse to stop shooting yourself in the foot, we shall also refuse to and, indeed, shoot ourselves in both feet, just to show that we are more serious. Such is the strange logic of 'reciprocity', the process by which liberalization of world trade proceeds – or, at present, doesn't. I parody only a little.

There are some plausible arguments for trade restrictions: to turn the terms of trade to advantage; or, more controversially, to protect 'infant industries'. But neither of these considerations is central to the current round of global negotiations, which have focused essentially on three issues: the need to produce some rules limiting the use of subsidies and trade restrictions in agriculture; the incorporation of emerging economies like China, India and Brazil into the processes of bargaining and reciprocal consensus that make up the trade negotiating process; and, as in every previous round of trade negotiations, to provide some forward momentum behind liberalization. The fear is that, without liberalization, the world might revert to the beggar-my-neighbour protectionism which didn't cause, but almost certainly deepened, the Great Depression.

The present round of negotiations was launched in the wake of 11 September 2001 and was designed to breathe optimism into the world economy when there was a fear that confidence would collapse. Seven years later, after repeated attempts to bring the negotiations to a satisfactory conclusion, they appear finally to have failed. The current global crisis, with its echoes of inter-war financial disorder, has made success in the negotiations more necessary but also more difficult.

The central issue in the negotiations has been agriculture, long insulated from post-war liberalization by the remarkable capacity of relatively small and dwindling numbers of farmers to hold governments political hostage in the EU, the USA and Japan. Some, limited, progress was made in earlier rounds of trade negotiations in isolating subsidies that are 'trade distorting' – that is, export subsidies – but in this round little progress has been made to reduce subsidies on an agreed basis or to reduce market access barriers. For this reason, there are potentially much larger gains from agricultural liberalization than anywhere else. One estimate is that a radical liberalization package would lead to a global economic benefit of $300 billion a year by 2015, even without additional productivity gains from competition. Agriculture accounts for 60 per cent of the potential benefits of the round, although agriculture and food processing account for under 10 per cent of world trade and 4 per cent of world GDP (though for a substantial majority of the world's population, if subsistence farmers were to be included).

In the event, the negotiations collapsed. There were several contributory factors. The European Union was seeking to limit farm liberalization as far as possible and, to the end, President Sarkozy was publicly demanding a curb on further offers by the EU trade negotiator, Peter Mandelson. The USA, which had traditionally led the demands for subsidy cuts, had insisted that its own commitment to farm spending should not be reduced (even though much of it had not been used hitherto). There was also resistance from developing countries such as India to reducing their own, high, tariffs and trade restrictions. Moreover, the final stages of negotiation coincided with a flurry of panic new trade restrictions in the face of rising food prices – including export controls in Argentina, potentially one of the biggest beneficiaries of a liberalization agreement. All of this underlined the crucial importance of an agreement, but also the political problems involved in achieving one: simultaneously resisting populist measures at a time when people were hungry and angry, and confronting powerful producer vested interests in pursuit of an international agreement the benefits of which would not always be obvious in the short run.

Finally, it was not agriculture that led to the ultimate breakdown in negotiations. Successive rounds of negotiation have progressively reduced tariffs on manufactured goods to low levels and removed most quotas. The new round was to take this process further: cutting EU tariffs from 10 per cent to 4.5 per cent, but also including trade barrier cuts from developing countries, albeit less substantial and over longer periods and with more exceptions. China's car tariff would go down from 25 to 18 per cent, for example. One complexity was that the negotiations were not about actual tariffs but about 'bound' tariffs (that is, cuts that cannot be reversed). What was being asked of governments was often not to expose industries to more competition but to restrict their freedom of manoeuvre in the future. In the event, there was a disagreement between the USA on one hand and India and China on the other as to how much the latter should liberalize in order to make the package as a whole work.

The fact that India and China were the catalysts of a breakdown was important, even though a breakdown might well have occurred anyway. While the long-standing arguments about agriculture between the USA and the EU are damaging and costly to their own citizens and many developing-country food producers, they do not involve any fundamental disagreement about the merits of trade. But in the reaction to India and China there are hints of a more profound discomfort with these countries' emergence as big players in international trade, and also a lack of commitment by these countries themselves, both of which have emerged from a long period of near autarky, to trade liberalization.

The discomfort in developed countries towards the big new Asian competitors stems from an underlying fear of the introduction of very large numbers of poor workers into a world economy already characterized by intense competition. Fear of 'cheap labour' has been a recurrent theme in the politics of trade. Populist demagogues have long exploited the fears of the white working class against this perceived threat to their livelihood, be it from India in the seventeenth century, Japan in the early twentieth century, or, more recently, Mexico, China and, now, India again. Not only are the politics primitive, so are the economics. Martin Wolf and others, including the author, have expended rivers of ink seeking to demolish the fallacies, of varying sophistication, that have engendered a protectionist approach towards trade with poor countries.

What has caused a more sceptical approach to the benefits of freer trade to re-emerge is concern over the distributional impact. It is one of the most basic propositions of trade theory, as already argued above, that specialization will increase returns to the relatively scarce factor of production. In other words, in a developed country trading with a poorer country with abundant labour, there would tend to be increased returns to capital and pressure on wages. The standard response has long been that these effects are in practice small and are swamped by the impact of technology, that those adversely affected can adjust into areas of employment not facing overseas competition, and that the overall benefits outweigh any costs. There has, however, been the emergence of evidence that returns to capital are growing and real wages are being squeezed. How far this is due to China's (let alone India's) entry into the world economy is debatable.

Until recently, Western leaders have been persuaded that it is desirable, and mutually advantageous overall, to welcome China and other emerging economies into a liberal global trade system. However, the increasingly widespread belief that import competition across a wide range of goods is depressing wages and employment has sapped the willingness and ability of governments to force through liberalizing legislation. There is now a major problem in the USA, with a hostile Democrat-controlled and union-influenced Congress. Even before President-elect

Obama takes centre stage, we have seen the absurd spectacle of a right-wing Republican president, with impeccable anti-union credentials, berating the Chinese (and other countries) for not upholding labour rights, and empathizing with American blue-collar workers over the unfairness of low-wage competition.

Should the trade talks have definitively failed, there are several likely damaging consequences, even if the world does not descend into outright trade warfare. The potential gains would, of course, be forfeited. There is a likelihood of increasing use of regional and bilateral agreements that incorporate discriminatory treatment of non-members. This is essentially what happened in the 1930s, when the major powers turned inwards to their protected imperial markets. There is also a likelihood that, with the authority of the WTO diminished, there would be increasing, unilateral use of anti-dumping duties and other measures directed at China and other emerging economies, with the dispute settlement processes of the WTO becoming less and less effective. The tensions unleashed by the current crisis would therefore weaken further the already fragile structures that provide some sort of governance for the world economy.

———

The conflict latent in the tensions over exchange rates, and deeper imbalances in savings and investment, and the inability of the established economic powers to come to an agreement with the newcomers over trade, do not bode well for the future. The concerns over 'security' unleashed by the oil and food price shocks have also created a new source of potential disputes.

The near-collapse of the Western banking system and the onset of recession have, however, in the short term at least, led to a more cooperative approach. The Chinese have been bewildered by the unravelling of the capitalist world's sophisticated financial architecture and alarmed by the spread of recession to their economy, but appear to recognize that it is in their interests to achieve global stability.

At the end of 2008 it was clear that both China and India were staring in the face of a global recession which was affecting their exports and the confidence of foreign investors (Brazil seemed least affected of the large emerging economies). Enough has happened so far to demolish the theory that China and India have become 'decoupled' from the economies of the Western world and could grow under their own momentum. There is even speculation that China, in particular, will face political upheaval as rapid economic growth stalls, precipitating serious unemployment. And, while India's more decentralized and democratic political structures provide stronger shock absorbers in a time of crisis than China's centralized authoritarian system, the commitment among decision makers to pursue rapid development could be undermined by internal sectarian divisions and conflict with neighbouring Pakistan. These possibilities lie in the realm of speculation. The greater likelihood is that, since both countries rely primarily on internal demand and have a capacity to sustain high levels of investment and output growth for years to come, there will only be a temporary, limited slowdown.

There could therefore be a continued shift in the centre of gravity of the world economy towards the East, as the newcomers experience a slowdown but continue to grow, while the developed world flounders in recession and a broken model of financial intermediation. It remains to be seen whether the cooperative mood can be sustained in the face of a painful cyclical downturn and a simultaneous shift in relative economic power.

6

The Reaction, the Reactionaries and the Response

Economic and financial crises cause pain. People get hurt; they lose their jobs, their businesses and their homes. Pain leads to anger. And anger produces a quest for scapegoats; victims need someone to blame. Out of today's series of interconnected crises, there will be some creative solutions, but, also, some bad ideas and ugly prejudices.

One of the earliest recognizably modern financial crises with major economic and political consequences was the collapse of the South Sea Bubble in 1720. It was a crisis not unlike that of today, albeit on a scale that reflected the more modest development of financial markets three centuries ago. That bubble, like today's, was, in effect, a vast pyramid-selling scheme which enriched the promoters greatly but left those who bought into the scheme exposed to the risk of collapse. Like today's property markets, the South Seas seemed to offer the prospect of infinite expansion. The cleverest minds of the day – indeed, of all time, like Isaac Newton – were persuaded by the compelling logic of exponentially growing wealth to part with (and lose) all their savings. When the bubble burst, the consequences spread far beyond Great Britain and a severe recession came in its wake. Angry rioters among London's unemployed weavers smashed windows and terrorized the capital's upper class. Some relief from the pain was achieved by a parliamentary enquiry which dreamt up imaginative punishments for the promoters, including sewing them into a sack with poisonous snakes and throwing them into the Thames. But the venomous political climate also led to legislation strengthening protectionist trade restrictions against Indian calico – wearing it became a crime – thus transmitting the crisis from Europe to villages in Bihar and Bengal.

When the much bigger crash of the early 1930s devastated stock markets and broke banks across America and Europe, leading to deep economic slump, conditions were created in which political extremism could flourish. Mussolini was already in power, but Hitler was undoubtedly helped by the enveloping economic chaos. Indeed, Italian Fascism and National Socialism, and minor variants like Oswald Mosley's British Union of Fascists, derived ideological legitimacy from the manifest failures of global capitalism. The USA also succumbed to economic nationalism, which culminated in the Smoot–Hawley tariffs of 1930 during the disastrous Hoover presidency. The European powers, including Britain and also the British Empire, particularly Canada, retaliated in kind. Mussolini embarked on countermeasures, such as restrictions on American car imports, with particular relish. There is continuing debate as to how much trade warfare contributed to the economic depression of the early to mid-1930s, but it certainly didn't help. In other parts of the world, the climate of economic nationalism reinforced the conviction of imperialists in Japan that the future lay with territorial expansion to secure markets and raw materials, which led to war.

———

It is not yet clear what form political reaction to the current crisis will take. But well before the current upheaval in financial markets there was what can loosely be described as an 'anti-globalization' movement. Its extreme manifestations were the violent demonstrations at or near big international economic summits, as at Seattle. They were motivated by different philosophical strands – anarchism, revolutionary communism, radical environmentalism – and a mixture of issues and causes: the lending conditions of the IMF; the World Trade Organization (WTO); 'unfair' trade, as seen from the viewpoint both of workers in rich countries and of farmers in poor countries; global warming; multinational companies, especially those in extractive industries; privatization in developing countries; human rights abuses; the foreign policy of the Bush administration; and many other of the world's real or imagined evils.

Except possibly in France, the anti-globalization protests never had any identifiable political core, but rather represented a ragbag of discontents. They were the angry fringes of political life: those who, for many different reasons, did not buy into the idea of the 'end of history' whereby political and economic liberalization were seen as inexorable and positive forces.

But it would be a mistake to underestimate the influence of those who give intellectual stiffening to the inchoate protests and who are now being listened to more attentively. George Monbiot, for example, has argued trenchantly against 'free trade', and articulates the concerns of many 'deep-green' environmentalists about the impact of international specialization, through trade and investment, and competition, on long-term sustainability. John Gray provided a conservative critique of the impact of internationally competitive markets on stable communities and national cohesion. (Marx, by contrast, was a free-trader, for the opposite reason: 'the protective system of our day is conservative while the free trade system is destructive ... [and] hastens the social revolution'.) Ethical criticisms were expressed by some of the churches, notably the Catholic papacy and Muslim scholars and activists, about the amoral (and sometimes immoral) activities of capitalist markets. There are those who did not lose faith in socialist analysis, from Noam Chomsky on the role of multinationals to Bob Rowthorn's work on the impact of immigration on British working-class concerns. Among the more original critiques is that of David Singh Grewal, who makes the case that globalization reduces rather than increases choice and diversity because of the dominance of network standards. None of this adds up to a coherent and consistent alternative view of how the world should be run, but there is now a small army of critics who can say 'we told you so'.

Even those who see the overall merit of globalization have nonetheless identified several economic and political factors pulling powerfully in the opposite direction. The first of these relates to the distributional impact of international economic integration. We have already referred to the academic and political arguments regarding the impact of competition in manufacturing and services from the big low-wage economies, notably China and India. Larry Summers, recently appointed to a key post in the Obama administration, has written of the threat to the 'global middle'. His argument is that a combination of low wages, diffusible technology and an ability to access global markets is having an enormous and rapid impact on living standards in these poor countries, while there has also been a 'golden age' for owners of scarce commodities (oil sheikhdoms), intellectual property (patents, copyright, trademarks), capital, and a strong brand or star quality. But it is less obvious how the people in the middle benefit. Summers points to the fact that median US family incomes have fallen far behind productivity growth, and average family incomes in Mexico have barely grown in the last – economically successful – decade and a half. He argues that without measures to win the support of the 'global middle class', it is 'very doubtful that the existing global order can be maintained'. It has to be said that there is little hard evidence that trade plays a central role in wage inequalities; and there are good studies, by Krugman and Lawrence among others, that suggest that trade with China either post-dated widening inequality or reduced it. But the intellectual climate has shifted in the opposite direction.

Underlying these debates is a fundamental question about who gains and who loses from an open, liberal economic system. The classic piece of economic theory that predicts outcomes is the Stolper–Samuelson model, which shows that in any one country it is the owners of the scarce factors of production (these being labour, capital or land) who benefit from protection, and owners of abundant factors who benefit from free trade. The model is stylized and hedged about with restrictive assumptions, but, in a rough and ready way, it helps to explain some of the main historical shifts we have seen. According to a perceptive analysis along these lines by William Bernstein, British 'free trade' came from a coalition of capitalists and workers uniting against a landowning oligarchy (land being scarce in this context). German Fascism came from an alliance of xenophobic landowners, capitalists and petty bourgeoisie against free-trading workers. The present line-up of interests in the Western world involves a clash between free-trading 'skilled' labour and protectionist unskilled labour (and, arguably, between mobile international companies and protectionist small business, with European landowners playing a familiar protectionist role). Suffice it to say that class rather than national interests explains much of what is happening in the policy debate.

Politically, too, the 'end of history' has not led to an uncontested liberal consensus – nor was it ever likely to. A decade ago I wrote about how the decline in socialism, at least in its more fundamentalist forms, would lead to a new polarity to replace the left–right divide. I argued that what would emerge would be a new emphasis on the 'politics of identity', a reaction to the forces of integration and globalization in the form of parties or wider movements emphasizing ethnic, religious or linguistic differences, or nationalism. There are many examples of how the politics of identity has come to the fore: in the USA, the 'culture wars' and the rise of the religious 'right'; in the UK, the importance and emotive force of immigration as an issue, the neuralgic issue of Europe, and the rise of Scottish nationalism; in India the emergence of the Hindutva and its political offshoot, the BJP, as a powerful party; the growth of Islamic radicalism; regional separatism in Spain, Italy and Belgium; anti-immigrant parties in Austria, Switzerland and the Netherlands; and the pathological extremes of ethnic politics in the former Yugoslavia and former Soviet Union.

Even before the financial crisis and global recession sent paroxysms of fear and uncertainty through many countries, there were already strong forces of reaction in place, and grievances based on perceived unfairness and inequality.

––––––––––

In the wake of the financial convulsions of 2008 and the deteriorating economic environment, we are beginning to see the shape of an emerging political reaction. In the EU, a book by the Italian finance minister, Giulio Tremonti, *The Fear and the Hope*, captures many of the fears of the working class and small business in a modernized xenophobia. He blames 'globalization' for the financial and commodity crisis. He is obsessed by China – 'the Chinese Dragon will possess Europe' – and claims to see a 'fifth column' of Chinese immigrants. It requires a particularly conspiratorial mind to see a sinister plan behind the Morecambe Bay cocklepickers and the growth of Chinese takeaways; but Tremonti identifies a potentially fruitful populist theme to enlarge upon as the centre of gravity of the world economy shifts towards China. Tremonti's prescription is more sophisticated than old-fashioned nationalism or fascism; it is 'Fortress Europe', albeit one finding common purpose in an 'Atlantic Area' with the USA. Some of these ideas are very similar to those advanced over a decade ago by Sir James Goldsmith in *Le Piège* (The Trap) and reflect ideas that are common among French, Italian and Spanish conservatives. They also tap into the instinctive statism of the Christian Democrat and nationalistic right, summed up recently by Nicolas Sarkozy: 'The market economy is a regulated market, a market that is at the service of development, and the service of society, and the service of all.' The practical application of this statism in a modern context is Sarkozy's proposal to set up a European sovereign wealth fund to buy up stakes in European companies (to keep out Arabs and Asians). Tremonti's wider appeal is to European 'identity' expressed through 'Judaeo-Christian' values. He may be a minor player in the wider scheme of things, but he has cleverly brought together a potentially potent – and dangerous – cocktail of themes: cultural identity; the new Europe; protectionism; fear of a rising Asia (and Russia).

In Europe, the voices of protectionism and the 'fortress' economy are drowned out, for the moment, by the more liberal and outward-looking tendencies of the Anglo-Saxon and Scandinavian worlds. But there are signs that in the USA similar ideas are gaining traction, as they have in periods of crisis in earlier generations. According to the Global Attitudes Survey in 2008, only 53 per cent of Americans think that trade is good for their country, as against 78 per cent in 2002 (compared with 87 per cent of Chinese, 90 per cent of Indians, 71 per cent of Japanese, 77 per cent of Britons and, surprisingly, 82 per cent of the French). In his election campaign, Barack Obama pledged to impose draconian labour standards as part of free-trade area agreements with the USA, and to introduce stronger controls into existing arrangements with 'low-wage' economies such as Mexico. There are powerful voices within the Democratic Party, which has a strong majority in the new Congress, urging the new administration to 'get tough' with China (after various anti-Chinese bills failed to make headway in the last Congress). One of the key battlegrounds within the new administration will be whether the 'liberal' critics of globalization are able to find liberal solutions – better healthcare and education, more redistributive taxation – before they are overtaken by the forces of economic nationalism.

Nor is American nervousness confined to trade. A Public Strategies Survey suggested that 55 per cent of Americans thought foreign investment harmed national security, and only 10 per cent disagreed. Resistance to Arab investment in US ports and Chinese investment in the oil industry – however small and innocuous – reflects a deeper disquiet, which will grow as the USA becomes more dependent on Middle Eastern and Asian sovereign wealth funds to recapitalize its battered financial institutions.

Although public opinion in most of the big new economic players appears to favour trade, the behaviour of governments suggests that there is a deep residue of nationalism in the economic policies of the emerging-market economies. While it is legitimate to criticize US and EU negotiators (and governments) for failure to offer more far-reaching concessions in liberalizing agricultural trade, it was India, supported by China, which, at the final moment of crisis, pulled the plug on the Doha Round of WTO negotiations. They were motivated not solely by frustration at the lack of progress surrounding open markets, but by a wish to protect their agricultural and financial sectors and anything that could be described as 'strategic'. In India, in particular, the conversion from earlier autarkic trade policies is only partial, and there are powerful voices on the Indian left and the nationalist right, as well as organized vested interests, vehemently opposed to opening up Indian markets. Policy debates in China are less transparent than in India, but it would be surprising if the heirs of Mao were anything other than deeply suspicious about opening up their economy too far. Even more than in the West, a preoccupation with 'economic security' – in relation to technology, food, energy and military hardware or software – is deeply ingrained. China has given aid to repressive regimes such as Sudan primarily in order to support state oil enterprises like Sinopec, reflecting a fusion of commercial and security concerns.

Russia cannot be blamed for the breakdown in the World Trade Organization – it is not a member and shows no great ambition to become one – but the newly assertive economic nationalism of Russia reflects a sense that national identity can be rekindled through economic success and aggrandisement, much as it was in Germany and Japan many decades ago. The war in Georgia and pressure on Ukraine reflect a brutal use of economic levers – oil and gas supplies – to influence foreign policy. A collapsing oil price may deflate Mr Putin's pretentions rather quickly, but the authoritarian, nationalistic capitalism he represents is a challenging alternative model which will appeal to many in the big emerging-market economies. China's approach to its trading and investment partners is altogether more subtle and less confrontational. Its state-controlled banks and sovereign wealth funds have been impeccably non-political and correct. But, in a few years' time, the flush of relative economic success combined with a reaction of defensive hostility in the USA and EU may make China appear more like Putin's Russia – and altogether more formidable with it. India, Brazil, Mexico and other emerging economies are not authoritarian, but their democratic capitalism has a strongly nationalistic edge.

The dilemma that is emerging is this. The free movement of goods, services, capital and, to a degree, people, has brought, and will bring, great economic benefits. The problems of globalization require cooperative solutions – over trade, environmental damage, pandemics and mass migration. Yet the strains on cooperation that are already apparent could become unsupportable in conditions of economic crisis. The Western world is increasingly looking inwards, and the new economic powers, which were never part of the multilateral order and therefore have no significant stake in it, are nurturing a nationalism of their own. The tension between globalization and rising nationalism is becoming extreme, and the outcome is not predictable.

———

The economic crisis has provoked a questioning not just of international integration – globalization – but of the whole private-enterprise system. The cry has gone up: 'self-regulation is finished', 'laissez-faire is dead', or 'the end of Thatcherism'. But the slogans mean different things to different people. The radical extremes of the 'green' movement or the 'anti-globalization' left, and some of the religious and ethical critics, never had any faith in the private-enterprise system and want to see it ripped down (though the nature of their alternative is usually unclear or deeply unappealing). Some of the more eloquent critics, like Larry Elliott and Dan Atkinson, make it clear that their alternative to a world run by the 'New Olympians' – the bankers and the intergovernmental organizations, the WTO, IMF and World Bank – is the restoration of post-war controls, together with a strong welfare state.

The current debate is often characterized by the use of the word Keynesianism. Keynes is often invoked; but, like many other great men, he said a lot of different things. He was, however, unambiguously a liberal (and Liberal), who wanted to save capitalism from itself. He wanted the market economy to work, and was dismissive of Marxist or highly interventionist ideas such as are being advanced by some of those now using his name. He was concerned primarily with what we now call macroeconomics, and with the necessity for the active use of monetary and fiscal policy to prevent downturns in the business cycle from spiralling further down – by pumping money into the economy through, for example, public works.

There is, in fact, little resistance to Keynesianism, in this narrow sense, today. The very prompt response to the current crisis by the US and UK authorities in particular reflected an essentially Keynesian view that in an emergency every lever has to be pulled – deep cuts in interest rates, fiscal stimulus, buying up 'bad assets' or recapitalizing banks – in order to maintain economic activity. There has been remarkably little dissent, though the rejection by the British Conservatives and the German government of a fiscal stimulus may open up a new debate.

The big debate that is taking place is on a somewhat different plane. On the one hand there are what I call the 'New Interventionists', who see the current disaster in financial markets – and thence in the wider economy – as essentially a product of excessively permissive, weak regulation: the Washington consensus of deregulation and privatization. On the other side are those who, for the most part, accept that there have been serious market failures but insist nonetheless that the present crisis owes more to bad or failed regulation than to markets, that the good markets do outweigh the bad, and that the costs of government failure often outweigh the costs of market failure. Let us call them the 'Old Liberals'. Within this dichotomy, there is a middle position – broadly that of the author – which acknowledges that financial markets are subject to repeated bubbles, panics and crashes, and maintains that they should not be confused with markets in goods and services within and between countries. The worry some of us have is that legitimate arguments for re-regulating financial markets will become confused with a generalized movement towards dirigisme and state control of economic activity.

At least in financial markets, the New Interventionists have a formidable charge sheet. Banks indulged in huge risks which took no account of entirely plausible scenarios of economic slowdown or contraction. Dangerously risky behaviour was reinforced through the bonus system; executives were rewarded with vast payments for running their banks into the ground. There appeared to be no regulatory control over massive leverage within investment banks – as much as 1:50 in some cases – or in 'shadow' banking institutions such as hedge funds. Controls over mainstream banks engaging in riskier investment banking were relaxed. The derivatives markets ran way ahead of any rules, and in the case of the $860 trillion credit default swaps market, without proper exchanges for settlement.

The Old Liberals have some good counter-arguments, though in the current political context they are perhaps too embarrassed to make them. They would argue that failures occurred as much in more-regulated markets, such as New York, as in those that were more permissive, like London. The crisis started and spread from the highly regulated US mortgage market – based on two state-created and regulated bodies, Fannie Mae and Freddie Mac – and arrived much later in the unregulated hedge funds (a large number of which have gone down without creating systemic damage or asking for a taxpayer bail-out). Recent financial crises have been most extreme in highly regulated, rule-bound systems, such as Japan. Much of the current crisis can be traced back to failures of the state, like the failure to use interest rates to 'prick' the property bubble; or to the unintended consequences of well-intentioned regulation, such as the Basle rules on bank capital adequacy, which prompted the growth of securitized markets, shadow banking and complex derivatives as means of avoiding them. Some of the more fatalistic Old Liberals, like Alan Greenspan, argue that whatever regulations are put in place, they will always be circumvented by market players who are more highly motivated than regulators. Other liberals, like Martin Wolf, argue that this is a 'counsel of despair'. This mainstream liberal view is not for laissez-faire but for better regulation, accepting that, in financial and other markets, success or failure must be rewarded or punished financially, and that, for all its flaws, no other system can work better. The liberal view is that there should be some regulation, but not regulatory overkill.

At present, this enormously important debate is largely hidden in subtle nuances rather than fundamental differences, since the reconstruction of the regulatory system is some way off. Few are disputing the need in the current panic for the state to take over ownership and control of banks; but a big difference will gradually emerge between those who see the takeover as a permanent mechanism for wielding state control, and those who see it as a transitional mechanism before (some form of) private ownership and financial markets are restored. Almost all are agreed that the state should rescue institutions that create problems of systemic risk, protect bank depositors, and help households faced with the threat of repossession. But there are big, underlying concerns among liberals that these interventions should be designed in such a way that they do not generate moral hazard: in other words, they should not encourage bankers, depositors or borrowers to repeat foolish and dangerous behaviour in the future, knowing that the state will always be there to cover for their mistakes.

Except on the marginalized fringes, there are few fundamentalists. No one seriously believes that the world would be a better place with Soviet-style, North Korean planning controls, and no one now seriously argues for market laissez-faire in financial or other markets. But it is clear that the balance has shifted within the mainstream debate. When the state has had to rescue the financial sector and the heroes of financial capitalism have been exposed as greedy fools, democratic politics is bound to reflect the shift in mood.

The issue for the future is that this change in mood could play out in different directions. One possibility is that the underlying commitment to liberal markets will remain, but with more attention to effective regulation of financial markets and more sensitivity to the casualties of change and to widening inequalities: what could be broadly described as a Scandinavian or Canadian response to the crisis. The early indications are that the Obama administration wishes to move in this direction. It is also the approach of the author, as will be clear from the concluding chapters.

The other response is one in which the state will retain a powerful controlling influence in the capitalist economy, in microeconomic as well as macroeconomic affairs, often acting in the name of 'economic security'. The succession of recent crises – from the energy and food price shocks to the financial crisis – increases the likelihood that there will be a move towards 'state capitalism' of the kind espoused in France and Italy, but potentially elevated to a European level. The emergence of what I called the 'new interventionism' reinforces the narrative that politicians and bureaucrats may not be perfectly qualified to manage economies, but they cannot do worse than the current malfunctioning markets and greedy, foolish financiers. Moreover, they will have an electoral mandate to act in the 'national interest'. By exercising effective control of finance, energy and agriculture in the interests of 'security', the state would thereby acquire a major role in the new commanding heights of the economy (and the collapse of advertising revenue supporting independent media might provide an unintended push in the same direction, strengthening the relative importance of state broadcasters, including our own BBC). Further legitimacy would be given to this state capitalism by the decline of socialism as a practical, popular ideology. Instead, the future could lie with businessmen who are able to align their interests with those of the state. Silvio Berlusconi is an extreme example.

The danger of an emerging state capitalism in Europe (it is less plausible in the USA and the smaller Anglo-Saxon countries) is that it is congruent with emerging economic structures in China, Russia and, in varying degrees, the other emerging economies, the oil-rich states and established Asian powers like Japan. Government-run energy companies from Saudi Arabia, Iran, Venezuela, Russia, China, India and Brazil control 80 per cent of world reserves of oil and gas. Russian and Chinese government entities look poised to dominate aluminium and iron ore. The typical financial institution is a state-owned bank or sovereign wealth fund, or a private body owned by a politically favoured prince or oligarch. The alignment of private and state interests promises all the worst features of capitalist economies – unfettered greed, corruption, and inequalities of wealth and power – without the benefits of competitive markets. State capitalism also dovetails neatly with an ideology of economic nationalism, which leads in turn to conflict over markets and resources, and makes impossible the cooperative solutions that are needed to deal with problems such as global warming. Fear and anger trump cooperation in a crisis. The inter-war world provides an awful warning as to the likely outcome when nationalism is the dominant ideology and state capitalism is the dominant economic structure.

There is, therefore, a major challenge to those who subscribe to a liberal view of economics, to work with those whose instincts are more social democratic and who wish to see better systems of regulation and strong social safety nets, albeit within a market economy and a framework of global rules. The new US administration clearly aspires to such a world and there are, still, influential allies in Europe and Japan, in the democratic emerging economies such as India and Brazil, and even among the more thoughtful elements of the Chinese bureaucratic elite. In the concluding chapter, I sketch out an agenda.

7

The Future: A Road Map

We are at the early stages of a financial and economic crisis of great severity and complexity, global reach and unpredictable political and social consequences. When I was paid for attempting to predict future economic developments for a leading multinational company, I was frequently reminded of the Arabic saying: 'those who claim to foresee the future are lying, even if by chance they are later proved right'. The extraordinary speed with which the crisis has unfolded and overwhelmed the unready should underline the need for caution in anticipating the next few months, let alone years. It is perhaps more helpful to think of plausible scenarios than likely developments, and to frame any policy proposals in a spirit of humility, recognizing that no one fully understands what is happening or how the current drama will play out.

What we do have is historical experience and the accumulated knowledge that follows from it. There is much wisdom in the adage that 'history is an imperfect guide to the future but it is the only one we have.' I have emphasized from the outset that economic history provides a long record of cycles – in goods and raw material prices, house prices and construction, manufacturing production, employment – and financial market manias and panics leading to banking crises. It is only extraordinary conceit and complacency that have shielded those who should have known better from recognizing the danger signs – most notoriously and eloquently in Gordon Brown's claim to have abolished 'boom and bust'. But a generation of bankers, regulators, government officials and politicians were no less culpable.

It is now broadly recognized that, barring an improbably sudden recovery, the current upheaval is much more serious in scale and scope than those experienced, at least in the developed world, since the Second World War. We should not forget, however, that some Asian countries suffered grievously from the financial crisis of the 1990s; there was an economic as well as a political collapse in the former Soviet Union (Russia and Ukraine experienced a decline of over 50 per cent of GDP), and the Latin American debt crisis of the 1980s inflicted major losses.

Parallels are now being drawn with the Great Crash and then the Depression of the 1930s. In the USA, by no means the biggest casualty of that period, GDP fell by 30 per cent from peak to trough and took a decade to recover 1929 levels. The 1929 share price crash and what followed were in some obvious ways different from, and worse than, anything that seems likely today. The current crisis has occurred after a decade – indeed decades – of rising prosperity and technological innovation, which provide a platform for recovery, unlike the inter-war world which was weakened by war, hardship, hyperinflation in some countries and political instability. The world today also has, at least for the moment, a dense network of international cooperative agreements covering trade, standard-setting, banking regulation and overseas investment. These may be flawed and inadequate, but they are far ahead of the pre-war world, which, despite the efforts of the League of Nations, was characterized by nationalistic hatreds and imperialisms. Another new development is the major impact on global demand of China, India and other emerging economies, which in the inter-war period were impoverished by civil war (China), colonial stagnation (India), or revolution and autarky (Russia). It is possible that these countries will be dragged under by the international financial crisis and global recession, but China and India, at least, have strong domestic demand and well-diversified economies. And, not least, there has been a rapid policy response to prevent a wholesale collapse of the banking system and to allow rapid cuts in interest rates together with fiscal expansion. A vast amount of economic firepower is now being deployed to counter the global recession, whereas in the 1930s governments dithered, endlessly pursuing what they thought were sound fiscal policies: balancing budgets and, in the name of market forces, allowing banks to go bust, thus deepening the systemic crisis. It is reassuring that the general now in charge of the armoury, the Chairman of the US Federal Reserve, made his professional reputation as a historian of the Great Crash and the policy response to it.

These are the optimistic factors that lead many commentators and political leaders to believe that the crisis will be relatively mild and will lead to recovery in a couple of years at most. Even if the analysis is wrong, optimism has intrinsic value as a source of consumer and business confidence, and it should not be blithely dismissed. It is worth recalling Dr Johnson's advice about over-reacting to economic crisis, as in the 'general distrust and timidity' that followed in the wake of the bursting of the South Sea Bubble in 1722: 'little more than a panick terrour from which when they recover many will wonder why they were frightened'. And it has always been the case that those at the centre of a financial crash see the world in more apocalyptic terms than those somewhat removed, in the real economy. The confidence of the British financial establishment, for example, has been shaken to the core, not merely by the humiliation of the run on Northern Rock but by the realization in October 2008 that British banks could no longer rely on overnight lending and faced total collapse. They were in the same position as was described in 1825 by William Huskisson, the President of the Board of Trade, who noted that 'if the difficulties had continued only eight and forty hours longer ... the effect would have been to put a stop to all dealing between man and man, except by way of barter'. It is possible – we do not yet know – that the current extreme anxiety in financial markets will reverse itself quite quickly, as in these earlier historical episodes.

But the current crisis could well be as threatening as the convulsions of the inter-war period. The financial system is more complex and more interconnected than in previous crises. The shocks are bigger and are being transmitted more quickly at home and abroad through instant communications. The extraordinary scale of the derivatives markets, many times bigger than the world economy, points to the risk of even greater financial shocks. The degree of leverage now being reversed is on a staggering scale, and the underlying global imbalances – notably between the savers and the spenders – will require long and painful adjustment. The pain to be faced – in unemployment, home repossessions and loss of savings – will produce a political reaction that could put at risk many of the post-war gains, such as international consensus over the merits of trade, which we have come to take for granted.

It is possible to envisage two broad scenarios. One is that the rapid policy response, and the necessary adjustments, will work, leading to recovery, but almost certainly after a deeper, nastier recession than the governments of the leading economies now expect. Another possibility, at least for some countries, is that the policy response will not work, because the problems, especially in the banking system, are too deep-rooted and difficult. Japan has never really recovered from its banking crisis of almost two decades ago, due in part to an unwillingness to acknowledge and deal with the losses to the banking system acquired in the property and land bubble of the 1980s. Lessons have been learned from the Japanese experience about the need for prompt, transparent intervention to sort out bad banks. Japan also taught us that a sophisticated, developed economy can be disabled for a long period as a result of a deep financial crisis, even when, in that particular case, it had the advantages of a benign international environment and a stable, quiescent political system.

The problems faced by some countries, especially Britain and the USA, are not just technical and economic, but represent a blow to the underlying value system, the social contract. Most people's sense of fairness and equity had already been assaulted by widening extremes of wealth and income. By 2007 the value attributed in assets to 'high net-worth' individuals (dollar millionaires) was three times greater than US GNP, and higher than the combined GNP of the G7 countries. The income of the world's richest 500 billionaires exceeded that of the world's poorest 420 million people. However, widening inequality of wealth and income – in the case of the UK income inequality is very close to, and wealth inequality greater than, that at the end of the Thatcher era despite redistributive measures – has been tolerated, and politically endorsed, because it appeared to be a consequence of economic progress. A rising tide lifted all boats, it was argued, even if the biggest boats derived the biggest benefit. The rich should get richer, because they were seen to be applying entrepreneurial talents that, apparently, benefited the common good – even if some of them were rogues. The richest man in the world, Bill Gates, did something useful, and was generous too. Even the less obviously useful people in the City of London or the New York markets, or Russian and Arab billionaires, who flaunted wealth of questionable provenance, were part of a success story that provided full employment and rising living standards.

That has now changed. A lot of people are getting hurt: hardworking, thrifty, law-abiding people. Many are losing their jobs, their homes and businesses. Shareholdings have been shredded and, with them, many defined-contribution occupational and private pensions. Yet the losers can see that some of those who made a fortune in bonuses brought their banks to their knees, and that those banks are now being rescued by the taxpayer. The reckless and incompetent are being rewarded, the prudent and socially responsible punished. Therein lies a great sense of unfairness. We do not yet know how this sense of grievance will manifest itself politically, but there is unlikely to be a return to the freewheeling ways of before the crisis.

———

What should be done? There are some who argue that nothing much should be done, that the crisis will, like a forest fire, in due course burn itself out, and that to intervene would prevent a necessary purge of past excesses. We know from the various interventions by the US Federal Reserve in the Greenspan era – the sharp cut in interest rates during the dot.com bubble and the Asian financial crisis – that one of the consequences was to encourage even more irresponsible lending practices than thitherto. Past guarantees given by governments have undoubtedly encouraged banks to operate with less and less capital and liquidity relative to assets. There are legitimate anxieties that the bail-out and rescues today will sow the seeds of an even bigger crisis in years to come. It is not difficult to make a theoretical case, based on moral hazard, for non-intervention. The influential Austrian school of economics, including great thinkers like von Mises and von Hayek, argued throughout the twentieth century that 'malinvestment' in previous boom periiods must be purged and liquidated without government intervention. Indeed, in earlier eras there was simply no scope for governments to intervene. There were automatic, rules-based, systems such as the gold standard that prevented governments from intervening in monetary policy. Non-intervention did not guarantee stability. But banks behaved very carefully, because they could go bust if they became insolvent. Economic cycles happened and bottomed out without active government intervention.

The 1930s spelled the end of that passive approach to financial and economic crises. In an era of universal adult political participation, it was increasingly politically impossible to accept mass unemployment or to force big wage cuts as the gold standard required. Whatever the economic niceties of Keynesian economics, and its critique of the Austrians, it started from a political assumption that societies would not accept a laissez-faire approach and that wages were 'sticky'. Equally, in the current context there is likely to be little support for the proposition that governments should stand by while a downward spiral develops of evaporating consumer and investor confidence, disappearing credit, large-scale bankruptcy, mass unemployment, collapsing housing and other asset prices, and home repossessions – in the quiet knowledge that at some point the economy will hit rock bottom and the spiral will go into reverse. Barack Obama has used the image that when a house is on fire and the fire is in danger of spreading across the neighbourhood, the fire brigade should not stand and watch in the hope of encouraging greater awareness of fire risk and discouraging foolish habits like smoking in bed.

At the time of writing, the fire is already of frightening proportions. And there is also plenty of combustible material around that could ignite at any time, fuelling the blaze. The house-price collapse has led to falls of 20 to 30 per cent in the UK and the USA. But UK house prices still have another 20 per cent or so to fall to a point where price-to-income ratios are at a sustainable long-term level. Moreover, markets usually overshoot. These further falls will add to negative equity and to the losses of banks.

Then there are commercial property, credit cards and car loans, which will bring a new round of defaults as recession mounts. The crisis is now spreading to leading corporates – the car industry, steel, construction, retail chains – and there will be numerous and high-profile bankruptcies, which will drag down suppliers and add further to the bad debts of the banking system. The fire is also spreading internationally to sovereign debt, with the most vulnerable countries already requiring emergency balance of payments support. Doubts about government borrowing are spreading from extreme cases like Iceland and emerging markets such as Pakistan to over-borrowed European countries such as Ireland, Greece and Spain, and are now beginning to affect the UK. And there are reports of trade being affected as long-standing trade credit arrangements for shipping are called into question.

———————

Firemen fighting a big blaze need to pour on lots of water. The first line of defence, and the orthodox, monetarist response to a contraction of credit, is monetary expansion through deep cuts in interest rates. Milton Friedman, no less than Keynes, would have argued for aggressive use of monetary policy. Only the austere 'Austrians' believe the opposite: that interest rates should rise to purge past bad investment. Monetary expansion is now being pursued in the USA, the UK, the eurozone, Japan, Sweden and elsewhere. The aim is to spur spending by reducing the cost of borrowing for firms and households. As inflation turns into deflation – and we are beginning to see falling prices and pay cuts – interest rates will, and will need to, fall towards zero. The world of deflation is something that has not been experienced in our lifetime, except, to a limited extent, in Japan. It is like a world of zero gravity in which all our assumptions about movement are turned upside down. Debts become more onerous, even if interest rates are very low. Conversely, cash savings become more valuable. Because prices are expected to fall, buyers defer spending until prices have fallen even further. Lack of spending adds to depression and further downward pressure on prices, while workers take pay cuts to save their jobs. Active monetary policy through interest rate cuts is necessary rather than sufficient, however. It cannot work any more once rates have fallen to zero, or if the public is so frightened that it hoards cash even when interest rates make it unattractive to save.

But even before we have reached that world, the active use of interest rates is proving a blunt, even ineffectual, instrument, because banks are not able or willing to pass on interest rate cuts to their borrowers. Banks are having to borrow at significantly higher rates than the central bank rate because the normal mechanisms of money transmission have broken down. Despite government money pumped into banks, and despite government guarantees on the money banks lend to each other, investors are still wary of putting their money into banks except at a premium, which raises borrowing costs.

There are other ways of stimulating the economy using monetary policy. The central bank controls the supply of money and can pump more money into the economy to encourage spending. It can do this by expanding the reserves of the banks, for the purpose of lending on to business or consumers. But in the current climate, banks are reluctant to draw on these reserves. They are also being pressed by other agencies – the financial regulators – to hold greater cash reserves, not less, and that reinforces the banks' new-found conservatism, avoiding risk wherever possible and reducing their loan exposure. Governments can bypass the banks altogether by lending directly to big firms (by buying up firms' short-term debt, as is happening in the USA), though this raises practical problems of the government acting as a lending agency and can really only work for very large firms. Alternatively, money can simply be printed and handed out to people to spend. I shall return later to the emotive issue of 'printing money' and the inflationary risks involved. But the practical problem in this context is that it may do little good if the money does not circulate but is hoarded because firms and families are scared to spend it. Nor does it deal with issues of insolvency in financial institutions, which are paralysed as a result.

Where monetary policy does not work, or work well, governments have to use fiscal policy: that is, government deficit financing, putting money into peoples' pockets via tax cuts or public spending, or both. That was the particular insight of Keynes. His magnum opus, the *General Theory of Employment, Interest and Money*, was in fact a specific theory designed to address the unusual circumstances in which monetary policy is not effective. His view, which has now become accepted wisdom almost everywhere, is that in these circumstances it is necessary to depart from the orthodox view that governments should aim to balance their budgets. Governments should borrow and spend in order to maintain the level of activity of the economy. In a modern economy, there is broad acceptance that deficits should be allowed to widen in a period of slowdown (because tax receipts fall and welfare costs rise), offset by surpluses in a cyclical upswing. But in a slump, Keynesian remedies go further than that and involve a calculated additional injection of purchasing power through deficit-financed tax cuts or spending, or both. That is what is needed – and is happening – now.

Keynes said many things, not all of them consistent. He has also been widely quoted in defence of positions he certainly did not hold. In the post-war era he was widely associated with a large-scale expansion of public spending, in totally different conditions from the inter-war period, and with unsustainable deficit financing, which led to inflation. The experience of the post-war era was that increases in public spending in bad times were not offset by contraction in good times, and that cumulatively excessive government borrowing drove up (long-term) interest rates and 'crowded out' private investment. As a result Keynesianism had become discredited by the 1980s. Furthermore, politically, Keynesianism was appropriated by socialists, though Keynes was not a socialist but a Liberal (and liberal), who was concerned with saving capitalism, not replacing it. Seven decades after he developed his ideas – in parallel with the ideas implicit in the American New Deal – circumstances have once again returned in which those ideas are highly relevant in their original form.

What governments have to do in these circumstances is temporarily to maintain demand, in order to stop a self-fulfilling economic slump, using the government balance sheet to borrow, while debt-laden companies and individuals recover confidence and rebuild their own balance sheets and reduce their debt. Public borrowing is currently cheap, because investors trust governments ahead of most private borrowers. The fiscal stimulus should do either or both of two things, putting money directly into the hands of consumers, or investing in a once-and-for-all programme of public-infrastructure investment which can be mobilized quickly: social house-building; rail and road projects for which the design and preparations have already been completed – what Americans call 'shovel-ready' projects. The Obama package put before Congress in January 2009 meets these requirements to the tune of around 4 per cent of GDP. The Gordon Brown stimulus package announced in November 2008 is proportionately more modest (just under 1 per cent of GDP) and the small, temporary cut in VAT is unlikely to do a great deal for private consumption because it is a drop in an ocean of retailer discounting.

Just as in the 1930s, the Keynesian remedy is proving controversial. British Conservatives and American Republicans have attacked such methods, as they did in that earlier crisis. Underlying some of this hostility is a philosophical position – the 'Austrian' view of economics – that recessions should purge themselves of past 'malinvestment'. Germans of all political stripes seem reticent about Keynesian policy, perhaps because their folk memory is that 'Keynesian' economics was the fiscal stimulus of Adolf Hitler's rearmament programme. One objection, currently advanced mainly by the German government, is that a fiscal stimulus does little good, since households will save more to compensate for government spending because they fear higher taxes or higher inflation later (so-called 'Ricardian equivalence'). There is even an argument that fiscal consolidation will raise consumption better than a fiscal stimulus, because consumers will revise upwards their estimate of permanent disposable income and therefore spend more. A related argument, used by Anglo-Saxon fiscal conservatives, is that deficit financing will inevitably be followed by higher taxes (or infation) in the long term, causing economic damage, and so should not be undertaken. Keynes's own answer to this point was that 'in the long run we are all dead': failure to act could produce a deeper slump and an even bigger fiscal black hole than if no government action were taken.

It is too easy to caricature the arguments about fiscal policy. A lot depends on the inherited fiscal position of the government, the expected longevity and severity of the recession, and the design of the policy package. There are some legitimate criticisms of what is called 'toxic Keynesianism': that the fiscal stimulus envisaged in the UK, particularly, may have the effect of depressing consumer and private-sector confidence, because compensating tax increases are clearly signalled and because the public may be unconvinced that a return to long-term fiscal discipline is credible. I have taken the view that in the current circumstances it is on balance right to attempt a fiscal stimulus, recognizing, however, the risks. The alternative – prolonged and deepening slump – would be worse.

Expansionary fiscal policy also has its limits and has to be treated with care. The bond markets, which the government use to borrow money, may resist new issues, forcing up yields and the cost of capital. Some governments are already finding it difficult to borrow, but while some highly indebted countries, such as Greece and Italy, pay a significant premium over US bonds, other highly indebted governments, like Japan, can still borrow very cheaply because they have access to willing domestic savers who trust government paper. Overall, there is no serious constraint at present on deficit financing through the markets, but it may well be coming.

Supposing, however, that conventional monetary and fiscal policy fails: what then? Japan struggled for a decade with prolonged recession brought about by a deflating property bubble and an overhang of debt. Fiscal stimuli and zero interest rates didn't work. One solution to this problem, were it to arise now in major economies, would be for governments directly to expand the money supply. The euphemism 'quantitative easing' is increasingly being used in the USA, and was advocated by Mr Ben Bernanke of the US Federal Reserve when Japan was mired in its crisis. Essentially, the government borrows from the central bank rather than the markets. The government, in effect, leaves its deficit unfunded. The money created could be used either to give money to individuals, bypassing banks and money markets, or to support and cheapen the government's market borrowing (by the government offering cash to buy up its own long-term bonds). Or it could be used to buy up a variety of private assets, including bad and toxic debt, in order to encourage new lending. Carefully managed, the inflationary impact of money expansion – which is popularly described as printing money though it does not directly involve printing presses – would simply offset the forces of deflation. The problem is, however, that governments might not know when to stop. They might be tempted to create inflation to revive the economy by rescuing debtors (at the expense of savers). Fears that governments might be headed down the road to Mugabe's Zimbabwe or the Weimer Republic could frighten currency markets and, of course, voters. The USA – and possibly the UK and the European Central Bank, too – appears poised to go down this route; but any government that does so will have to take care to ensure that there is no excess money created, or that it is mopped up quickly (which could require government borrowing by the issuing of bonds).

The measures above, of varying degrees of radicalism, are designed to stimulate economies that are in recession, or worse, and suffer lack of purchasing power because consumers have been frightened or impoverished, or persuaded by bad experience of personal indebtedness to be prudent. Such policies are, unfortunately for politicians, counter-intuitive. It is 'common sense' to believe that in bad times families should be more careful and should spend less. Having seen the country's economy brought to its knees by a surfeit of indebtedness and profligacy, few people outside the rarefied groves of economic academe will easily be persuaded that it makes sense for the government to go on a spending spree or to encourage individuals to do the same. Therein lies the 'paradox of thrift': that prudent saving behaviour by individuals may be collectively damaging. Keynes may have persuaded his intellectual contemporaries of the need to confront the paradox through reflationary monetary and fiscal policies; it is the difficult job of politicians to win that argument in a democracy.

––––––––

Banks are also, on a massive scale, posing the paradox of thrift. Having been taken to the brink of, or over, the edge as a result of indulging in excessive leverage, and having inadequate capital to support the risks involved, banks are now furiously piling up capital reserves against bad debts, and restricting lending. As the Governor of the Bank of England observed recently of British banks: their behaviour is individually understandable but collectively suicidal – suicidal because they are dragging down the British economy, precipitating more bankruptcies and more bad debts for the banks themselves.

In order to break this destructive cycle, governments have followed a variant of the British model of bank capitalization. Late in 2008 the UK government injected large sums – £37 billion – to provide fresh capital, as well as guarantees for inter-bank lending. The purpose was to restore confidence in the banks by ensuring that they had enough capital to absorb any bad losses and to facilitate new lending. Barclays raised capital separately from the government but on more expensive terms, from Arab investors at an effective cost of 16 per cent.

Three months after the recapitalization there is still no sign of a return to 'normal' banking behaviour. Banks have been berated for reluctance to lend, but simultaneously have been required (by the financial regulator) to maintain strong reserves and also to repay the government investment as quickly as possible. However much bank managers may have been guilty of irresponsibility in the past, they now have conflicting objectives. It is the job of government to clarify which is the most important.

What else can be done? Is the only solution to wait until confidence gradually returns? The problem with waiting is that in the meantime good, solvent companies will be dragged down, along with others that are not sustainable, because they cannot renew their lines of credit. One possibility is further bank recapitalization, but this would involve yet more taxpayers' money, with a continued uncertain outcome. There is a danger that the government would be drawn into a succession of recapitalizations in order to deal with continuing crises as plunging asset prices devalue bank assets, swallowing up the capital that is put in.

Instead of, or alongside, further recapitalization, I believe that governments will have to treat the banks as if they were nationalized and require them to keep lending to solvent customers, recognizing that there may be some bad debts as a result. There is a real dilemma here. There is, on the one hand, little appetite, at least in the USA and UK, for civil servants to take over the banking role of assessing risks as between different borrowers, or for government to take on formal financial responsibility, as in the case of outright nationalization. In the UK, majority state ownership of RBS/NatWest and minority ownership of Lloyds/TSB has meant that there is a narrowing debate between 'nearly nationalization' and outright nationalization. The latter takes the government further, and reluctantly, into the direction of lending but it provides clarity, the means to bring hidden bad debt into the light and an opportunity to ensure new flows of credit (as is now, belatedly, occurring through Northern Rock). In any event, government cannot now walk away. It has no alternative but to keep the banks performing their role of transforming short-term assets into long-term loans, until a more fundamental reform of the banking system can be introduced after the crisis. At the very least, government nominees to the boards of rescued banks should be directing strategy, though not micromanaging the banks.

Other steps have to be taken to remove bad and toxic debts from the banking system. The Paulson plan in the USA was designed to remove bad debts from balance sheets, by buying up toxic loans through market mechanisms. That particular programme hasn't worked, but the concept remains valid. The most successful programme for managing a bank crisis – through the Swedish Bank Support Authority in the early 1990s – involved bank recapitalization but also the separation of 'good' and 'bad' assets, following the forced disclosure of problem loans, into 'good' and 'bad' banks. The latter were actively managed in order to reduce losses, and the former prepared for (profitable) privatization. The Swedish model is not entirely applicable today, because the crisis was limited to Scandinavia and took place in a benign international environment. But the key elements – recapitalization, the creation of a 'bad bank', active state management pending reprivatization of a reformed, restructured system – provide the best template available.

There is one other element that may have to be adopted: additional measures to encourage new lending, either direct lending that bypasses the banks or, alternatively, state guarantees for new lending. As to the first, an element of this is happening already in the USA with Federal Reserve loans to large companies. But the state cannot create quickly and competently a new structure for lending to hundreds of thousands of small and medium-sized companies in parallel with the banks; nor should it need to. There are also elements of state guarantee already in the credit system – notably for export credit – and, in principle, this could be extended to facilitate new credit flows. This idea was adopted by the UK government in its January 2009 proposals. But it is not just a technical fix; it has radical implications. What is being proposed is nationalization, or part-nationalization, of credit: easier to manage institutionally than the nationalization of banks, but creating the same – vast – degree of contingent liabilities for the state (without the potential benefit from eventual disposal of nationalized assets) and the same responsibility for credit allocation. A variant of this idea, being applied in the USA, which avoids the state being directly involved in credit allocation, is for the government to buy up loans in the secondary market and mortgage back securities or the debt itself.

To escape from this crisis will require a combination of the above: more recapitalization of banks, forced lending, 'bad banks' perhaps, and lending guarantees. Different countries will require a different mix and approach, depending on the severity of the banking crisis. But, in each case, the price for restoring financial stability will be a greatly increased role for the state in the banking sector. That is, however, merely a short-term fix. After the crisis there will have to be a new regulatory regime providing better protection against systemic risk .

————

After the calamities of the last year, few now question that the Anglo-Saxon model of finance was deeply flawed, unstable and unsustainable. It will have to be remade in ways that greatly reduce the systemic risk from large volumes of excessively leveraged transactions, but that, hopefully, preserve the capacity for innovation. There is a balance to be struck. There is no attraction in a regime of vigorous exercise which then causes a massive heart attack. Nor is there merit in petrified immobility because the body is permanently attached to thermometers and assorted health-check devices.

There are those who dream of returning to a simpler, purer world in which there is genuinely competitive banking, no state involvement and no moral hazard. But that isn't going to happen, because the political will would fail at the first major crisis. We no longer live in the nineteenth century. Sophisticated, modern financial markets have become, in many respects, a public good, providing not just conventional banking but a system for pensions, house purchases and industrial finance that, in today's democracies, will not be allowed to collapse. A better approach is to say that since key firms cannot be allowed to fail, they must be more effectively regulated.

The rejoinder has been that more regulation will never work. Regulators were too slow to spot the problems involved in syndicated lending in the 1970s, for example. Cynics argue that if new rules are put in place, financial institutions will find a way around them. Indeed, the development of SIVs and other vehicles for securitized debt, off balance sheets, was generated in part by a wish to avoid capital adequacy regulations. Or bankers will simply stop trying to run their businesses in the interests of shareholders and customers, and concentrate on box-ticking. Or, even if there is a glaring new problem sitting in front of them, regulators will not see it or act upon it – as occurred with Northern Rock, which was subject to rules written by supervisors who did not appreciate the significance of the bank having no defence against a breakdown of its business model. A major government agency was created to oversee the two US housing-finance giants, Fannie Mae and Freddie Mac, but it failed to spot the problems. I repeat here, in parody form, the weary defeatism of those who say that there is no alternative to allowing the financial sector to lurch from boom to bust to boom, generating vast profits in the booms and liabilities for the taxpayer in the busts.

I agree with the analysis of Henry Kaufman, Martin Wolf and the economically liberal commentators who dismiss this negativism as a counsel of despair and argue that the greater the commitment to free enterprise the greater the need for regulation, since without it there is excessive instability among the institutions that are needed to finance the private sector. Smarter members of the financial community are already looking at how to ensure more effective regulation because they realize that there will be a clumsy regulatory backlash from governments if they don't define the reforms themselves. For example, initiatives are being taken in London by hedge funds and private equity to become more transparent. The three main rating agencies are also anxious to promote voluntary reform, knowing that they also could become scapegoats in the wake of the unrealistically high ratings they gave to many of the collapsed market instruments and institutions. They have recently been heavily criticized by the US Securities and Exchange Commission because of the conflict of interest built into their operations (clients whose insurance is rated also pay the rating agencies their fees). There is, at first sight, some attraction in self-regulation rather than more expensive and intrusive statutory regulation. Unfortunately, even if self-regulation is sincere and well-intentioned, it focuses on the behaviour of individual companies, whereas the problem is one not just of ensuring that firms adopt good practices but of addressing industry-wide, systemic risk.

There are three areas in particular where a reformed regulatory regime focused on systemic risk would make a difference. The first is to use the regulatory instruments available to reverse the pro-cyclical bias of current rules. Banks are required by law to apply international rules agreed in Basle, through the Bank of International Settlement, which govern the capital they hold in reserve. These rules are applied internationally, so as to prevent individual countries from trying to secure a competitive advantage for their banks by demanding less reserve capital than those in other countries. The rules are necessary, but they have operated, in practice, to reinforce booms and busts. In periods when bank lending is booming, market prices tend to understate risk, which is why excessively risky lending takes place, yet market prices are also used to assess capital requirements. Conversely, in an asset market collapse, market prices may exaggerate the loss in value, but they are also used to assess vulnerability and require banks to cut back their lending when they are already under pressure. If there is a market failure, the methods used to assess capital requirements compound that failure. Goodhart and Persaud have suggested how a counter-cyclical policy might work. There is already some practical experience of operating what they call 'dynamic provisioning', which is a counter-cyclical system that has helped to keep Spanish banks insulated from some of the impact of the recent crisis (Santander has emerged sufficiently strongly to add Alliance & Leicester to its UK portfolio, which already includes Abbey). We should, however, not be too carried away by the Spanish experience. Spain has had a property boom and bust at least as extreme as that in the UK.

A second theme, along the same lines, is that macroecomic policy, particularly monetary policy, should operate to deal with asset prices as well as inflation, conventionally measured through the consumer price index (CPI). There is a long-standing economic argument, going back to Irving Fisher almost a century ago, to the effect that measures of inflation should include assets. The practical argument is that if interest rates were used to target asset prices, bubbles could then be 'pricked' before they became dangerous. The orthodox view, advanced by Alan Greenspan in particular, is that bubbles cannot be satisfactorily identified, and the role of interest rate policy has to be restricted to cleaning up deflationary damage when a bubble bursts. There are genuine problems in assessing the degree of over- or undervaluation of asset markets, but the Swedes have, with some success, used interest rates to 'lean against the wind' and damp down the risk of another bubble wrecking their banking system, as occurred in the early 1990s. Sushil Wadhwani, a former member of the Bank of England's Monetary Policy Committee, has set out how such a system could operate more widely.

The measures described above fit within a framework of stronger 'macroprudential' policy that the Bank of International Settlements has been urging in the interests of financial stability. There is another area in which stronger regulation almost certainly has a role to play: that of remuneration and incentives. There is undoubtedly a good deal of resentment and cynicism generated by the economic rewards, particularly bonuses, paid in the financial services industry. To the extent that the problem is one of perceived unfairness, it can be better dealt with through taxation rather than regulation of pay. But there is a deeper argument that the system of remuneration based on bonuses encourages excessive and dangerous risk-taking, which adds to systemic instability. Since there is unlikely to be voluntary restraint, regulation should insist upon systems that are already good practice in many companies, with bonuses paid in stock that is not redeemable for some years.

In addition to regulatory reform, there are necessary changes in tax rules to reduce the unintended consequences of policy. The USA provides mortgage tax relief, which encourages over-borrowing. The UK provides business with interest tax relief, which encourages excessive leverage. Such practices will have to be reformed.

One of the trickiest but most important areas ripe for reform is the structure of the banking system itself. Nothing has caused more damage in the UK and the USA than the involvement of what used to be localized and specialized retail banks in global investment banking. Investment banking has, in recent years, resembled a casino, and the massive scale of gambling losses has dragged down traditional business and retail lending activities as banks try to rebuild their balance sheets. The folly – and conflict of interest – in allowing the managers of banks to acquire equity interest in corporate clients, financed by loans from an in-house commercial bank, was recognized after the Great Crash and led to the Glass–Steagall legislation of 1933, separating investment and commercial banking. These lessons were forgotten, and this was one aspect of modern financial liberalization that had dire and almost entirely negative consequences – as did the demutualizaton of building societies in the UK. This liberalization now has to be reversed. The sheer scale of the balance sheets of 'British' banks such as Royal Bank of Scotland/NatWest and Barclays – both of which have assets and liabilities bigger than the whole of the British GDP – is a reminder of how their business decisions impact so powerfully on the UK economy, and how their errors have inflicted widespread damage.

There are several kinds of banking structure that could emerge from this crisis. One is that banks, in future, could resemble utilities, like water companies. They would become essentially national, not international, institutions, servicing business and individual borrowers in return for 'lender of last resort' protection. They would be closely regulated and subject to statutory codes of conduct, allowed to earn a utility rate of return, and discouraged (or forbidden) from venturing into investment banking and other high-risk activities. Bank managers would be incentivized to be reliable, predictable and boring, but also accessible. Financial wizards and thrill-seeking risk-takers would be free to participate in non-retail institutions such as hedge funds, which, quite explicitly, enjoy no government protection.

An alternative model is that there could be open competition, with bank licences available to a wider range of institutions – retailers, mutuals, as well as established banks – which would be free to attract deposits, provided that they satisfied a regulatory test of fitness (that is to say, they are not crooks, tax evaders or straw men). There would be full protection for depositors, but none for the institutions and their shareholders. Such a model would correspond more closely to a free-market situation, albeit with depositor protection. A more sceptical view is that, whatever prior assurances were given or refused, the government of the day would be bound in practice to rescue major, apparently systemically important institutions, as the Americans have done with AIG, Fannie Mae and Freddie Mac, and the British with Northern Rock and Icesave. All of which suggests that, in the real world, governments will necessarily intervene, and they should accept this from the outset and move towards the treatment of banks as regulated utilities.

The immediate priority is to protect the system from meltdown. But there has to be some link between short-term fixes and long-term structures. There is a real risk that governments will put taxpayers' money into the banking system without banks, or the public, having any clear sense of where long-term policy is heading and, in particular, what kind of banking industry should and will emerge. Clarity over the reform agenda is therefore urgently needed.

To introduce reforms of this kind in one country will be difficult enough. But financial markets no longer operate in narrow national silos. Financial markets are complex and entangled, and do not operate within national frontiers. So any meaningful regulatory response has to involve cooperation between the main regulatory authorities in the USA, the eurozone, the UK, Japan, China and perhaps more widely. Otherwise, there would be an open invitation to engage in regulatory arbitrage. We are, moreover, dealing not with some technical breakers of rules within a consensual framework, but with something much deeper: a collective collapse of confidence and trust, arising from an orgy of greed, a feeding frenzy of inflated fees and fantasy profits. It is tempting to enjoy the spectacle of some of the participants having their reputations, if not their personal fortunes, trashed. But it is neither feasible nor desirable for the system of modern finance to be destroyed. Information technology cannot be uninvented any more than nuclear technology. The vast, complex global structure of derivatives that are designed to spread risk still stands. Unlike the Twin Towers in 2001, it has not collapsed with the impact of the credit crunch, though serious damage has been done. We are still left with a series of interconnected markets, which were valued by the Bank of International Settlement in 2007 at $516 trillion, thirty-five times the size of the US economy in GDP terms, ten times the total size of the world economy, five times the size of all the world's stock and bond markets, and seven times the size of all the world's property markets. It has been called a shadow banking system. The problem remains of how to prevent a rogue 1–2 per cent of the market going wrong, the equivalent of a Pakistani nuclear weapon going astray. The only practical way in which such controls can be meaningfully introduced is through internationally agreed rules governing capital requirements and transparency for securitization and structured finance products and hedge funds. The challenge in terms of cross-border cooperation is immense.

The world of international finance is characterized by what Richard O'Brien called 'the end of geography': a high level of interconnectedness and rapid cross-border flows of money and data. The 'end' is, in practice, rather less definitive, because many less developed, emerging economies are not fully integrated financially with the rest of the world and, in all countries, there are numerous financial transactions that depend upon proximity and personal relationships. There is, nonetheless, a tension between the globalized world of financial and wider economic integration and the world of national political decision-making.

That tension is partly eased through agreed global rules. Long before this crisis, it was understood that the benefits of trade in goods and services and cross-border investment could not be realized without a rules-based global regime that embedded some common standards. There are, already, quite explicit Bank of International Settlement global rules governing bank capital requirements and, arguably, without these, banks would have become even more highly leveraged than they have been in pursuit of competitive advantage. There are the (less developed and self-regulatory) rules under the International Organization of Securities Commissions (IOSCO) governing global markets in securities, or the attempts being made to create common accounting rules. And the WTO not only liberalizes trade but also seeks to create rules for the fair – that is to say, equal – treatment of companies investing overseas and governing the use of subsidies. These transnational rules – some intergovernmental, some private sector – are fundamental to making globalization work.

There is some recognition, too, that one country's economic policies spill over on to others' through the activities of the International Monetary Fund – though, apart from emergency and politically onerous balance of payments assistance, mainly to small, poor countries, the IMF's formerly central role in easing countries' temporary payments crises has become peripheral. Instead of collaborating to provide a pool of funds to finance emergency lending, nervous governments have taken to insuring themselves by piling up large foreign exchange reserves: a wasteful alterantive which has added to global instability. The one major international structure to take account of cross-border policy impacts is the European Monetary Union and its accompanying fiscal rules (and also its important competition policy and state-aid rules). These limited and inadequate activities collectively represent the cooperative infrastructure, the flood defences, that have to withstand the stresses and strains of the massive storm currently hitting the global economy.

As we noted in the last chapter, there are strong political and institutional pressures to act in a nationalistic, not a competitive, manner, and an emerging 'state capitalism' that puts state actors at odds with international rules. So far, however, the main governments have acted on the principle that unless they hang together, and cooperate, they will hang separately. The European Union, the Group of 8 developed countries (and Russia), and the Group of 20 developed and major emerging countries have all been pressed into service, as never before, to produce agreed positions and action. In October 2008 the European Union narrowly avoided a beggar-my-neighbour competitive scramble for bank deposits, when Ireland and Greece offered unlimited depositor protection and other countries looked set to follow, before a common approach was agreed. The US Paulson plan and the British bank recapitalization plan were endorsed by each of the main countries affected by the banking crisis, and a version of the British plan was widely adopted.

There has also been a degree of commonality in the approach to new economic policy. At the height of the banking panic in October, there was an agreed 1 per cent cut in interest rates, partly to maximize the impact on business and consumer confidence, and partly to stop unilateral action triggering a currency crisis as markets targeted relative weakness. But Britain's more aggressive approach to interest rate cuts – and the perception that Britain is exceptionally vulnerable because of the size of its banking sector and the scale of its housing bubble – has already contributed to a serious weakening of sterling. Fiscal policy is more difficult to coordinate because it is difficult to compare the impact of different combinations of tax cuts and current and capital spending increases, and because measurements are only roughly consistent. Nonetheless, a loosely coordinated package was agreed in December 2008, which involves the USA providing a stimulus of around 4 per cent of GDP, mainly in public works. The EU is contributing around 1–2 per cent of GDP – despite big differences between member states and a strong reluctance to participate on the part of Germany. Other stimulus packages, from China and Japan, are ambitious but not entirely believable. And, so far, the main countries have resisted the temptation to indulge in protectionist trade policies and competitive industrial intervention. In particular, the refusal of the US Senate to countenance a bail-out for the car industry was a remarkable, unexpected and welcome act of self-discipline (showing a shrewd understanding of just where such policies might lead).

So far, so good. There is, however, one set of issues that is being addressed only tentatively and that has the capacity to derail any kind of cooperative response and to generate serious conflict. It concerns the shift in the centre of gravity of the world economy to the east, particularly to China, and the imbalances that have grown up, with China (and other surplus savings economies) providing large flows of capital to the USA (and the UK). As described in Chapter 5, the continued growth of the USA, based on imported savings and cheap finance, lay at the heart of the banking (and associated housing) crisis. And this growth was only possible, in turn, because of a system of 'vendor finance' provided by China to the rest of the world in order to enable Chinese exports to grow rapidly, fuelling Chinese economic growth.

By agreeing to participate in a common approach to fiscal stimulus, the Chinese are signalling a recognition that they can only continue to coexist peacefully (in economic and, perhaps, military terms) if their model of economic growth shifts towards domestic demand rather than export. Ominously, however, the Chinese authorities have responded to a serious slowdown in growth and export demand by pushing their undervalued exchange rate lower, rather than higher. And the Chinese official reading of the crisis has been in terms of Western – specifically US – economic weakness and lack of financial discipline, rather than a recognition of shared responsibility and mutual weaknesses. As the crisis deepens in 2009, there are American and European politicians aplenty spoiling for a fight with China: an economic war characterized by trade restrictions and a search for 'economic security' through bilateral deals and attempts to pre-empt supplies of energy and food. That would be a route to disaster.

There is an alternative: a new multilateralism that recognizes the changing balance in the world economy and has Asia at the heart, not at the edge of it. The references by many commentators to a New Bretton Woods agreement correctly emphasize multilateralism, but with it comes nostalgia for an Anglo-Saxon-led world with its intellectual capital somewhere on the civilized east coast of the USA. The New Bretton Woods, if it were to happen, would be better hosted in Singapore. The key participants would be the USA, China, Japan, the eurozone and India. The key issues that it would have to address, and resolve, are well-enough recognized and have already been the subject of innumerable conferences and speeches. This is not the place to rehearse all the complex issues involved, some of which have been dealt with above. But unless the key players can demonstrate a capacity to make serious headway on them, the existing structures could swiftly unravel, to be replaced by confrontation and conflict.

The first of the issues is the left-over business from the old Bretton Woods – exchange rates, economic imbalances, and macroeconomic stability – which has a new dimension in the surpluses of China (and other Asian and oil-exporting countries) vis-à-vis the deficits of the USA (and others). The IMF was to have been at the centre of the adjustment process. In practice, adjustment has been privatized, disastrously, and the international banking system has collapsed under the weight of it. The IMF, with quotas and voting weights radically changed to reflect the new economic reality, will have to have a much bigger role again, monitoring trends and coaxing governments with serious indebtedness, providing balance of payments finance that is adequate and timely, and overseeing the stronger regulatory regime for global finance that will emerge from the crisis.

Second, there is man-made climate change. Little progress can be made without fundamental agreement on the principle of 'contraction and convergence', as between the high-income countries, which have generated the lion's share of the stock of carbon in the atmosphere, and the big low-income countries, which will contribute the greatest future emissions. Without China or India as full and equal partners in the process, it will fail.

Third, there is revival of the stalled talks on world trade, which have ground to a halt, in substantial part because of lack of agreement on the most fundamental of traded goods: basic foodstuffs. The necessary opening of markets and the removal of damaging subsidies – as for biofuels – also has to reflect a legitimate concern in poor countries that there will be 'food security', and recognition that a large part of the world's population – the poorest – are peasant farmers engaged in subsistence farming or producing small marketable surpluses.

Last but not least, the development agenda – to eliminate hunger, poverty and disease – for which the World Bank is the lead agency, has to remain central, for both economic and moral reasons. Looking back on the events of the last few months, what is striking is the alacrity with which the USA and the EU have managed to mobilize $3 trillion (and rising) in capital and guarantees for failed banks, having failed to mobilize $300 million to help fight hunger in the midst of a food supply crisis earlier in the year. Such narcissistic self-absorption and twisted priorities do not bode well; but a structure of global governance in which the main emerging economies have parity would do something to redress the balance.

Postscript

This narrative of a global financial crisis began with the failure of a small bank based in Newcastle upon Tyne. I return to the north-east of England since it provides a fitting point of exit too. A few miles down the road from Newcastle is a jealous rival for the loyalties of the region, Sunderland. And just outside Sunderland is the Nissan car plant. The Nissan plant is the pride and joy of modern British manufacturing, arguably one of the most efficient car factories in the world, combining sophisticated technology with Japanese management and a flexible, committed British labour force which has retrained and moved on from the collapse of the old metal-bashing industries. Yet in the new year of 2009 Nissan closed its doors and sent its workers home because there was nothing for them to do. Its competitively priced and high-quality vehicles had no buyers. Excesses in mortgage lending first seriously exposed at Northern Rock had, over a mere fifteen months, spawned a global slump in demand for the products of the largest segment of manufacturing industry: the car industry.

I have described above the global linkages that led from the one to the other. But there is a particular significance for Britain. After the sense of defeatism and national decline of the 1970s, the painful transformation under Mrs Thatcher and then the decade of growth under a New Labour government had produced a new sense of national confidence, a confidence derived above all from having an economy that seemed to work well. Britain (at least in its own eyes) was elevated from the 'sick man of Europe' to an exemplar of good economic management, stability and contentment. No more 'boom and bust'. No more sterling crises. No more bloody-minded unions, decrepit factories or lagging growth rates. Even as the crisis has unfolded, the government has stuck uncompromisingly to the line that any problems are 'global', that the British economy is sound.

When we look at the foundations of this confidence it rested, essentially, on three main elements: the success of the global financial services industry, centred on London but of which Northern Rock was a provincial outpost; an openness to overseas investors as a source of technology, management and capital; and a sense of personal prosperity and well-being deriving from appreciating property prices for home owners and consumption, financed by borrowing. Yet, until the current crisis, these foundations had not been seriously tested.

In a big storm, even the finest-looking trees come down if they have shallow, insecure roots or an excessive weight of leaves. So the British economic miracle of recent years has been exposed as structurally unsound, however superficially impressive the foliage might have appeared. The effects on politics and national morale will be profound and long-lasting. Each of the key elements in the British 'success story' needs to be re-examined afresh. Starting with the last, the great housing bubble has provided an illusion of wealth and fed a lie: that housing equity is a safe form of saving, a pension, a one-way-bet. Many have been complicit in that lie: politicians, bankers, financial advisers and journalists. There are strong pressures to perpetuate the lie, to reflate property values through state-generated mortgage loans and other protections. And it may be that there will be some vindication for property investors, since the collapse of the house-building industry is destroying potential supply and helping to ensure that eventually, once demand recovers, prices will escalate because of supply bottlenecks. But the housing bubble, and associated personal (mortgage) debt has exposed a serious failure in economic policy: the failure of a much-vaunted independent central bank to manage asset inflation, and now deflation. The deeper challenge is to demystify property ownership and owner-occupation and to ensure that in future first-time buyers enter the market when prices are at more realistic levels and on the basis of a substantial deposit, and for government and local planners to aim for a much better mix of social, privately rented and owner-occupied property, as in Germany or Switzerland.

The property 'bubble' was, in turn, a consequence and a symptom of a wider and deeper problem: the spilling over into the British banking system of an excess of liquidity originating in cheap foreign money. Britain has had declining rates of household saving for over a decade – from 7 per cent of disposable income in 1998 to under 3 per cent in 2008 – and has imported savings from overseas. Rising living standards were maintained by household borrowing. Another way of putting the same thing is to say that Britain has been running current account deficits financed by imported capital. Since Nigel Lawson's economic boom in the late 1980s, under Mrs Thatcher, it has become fashionable to regard the balance of payments as of no great interest: merely an accounting identity which adjusts automatically through capital flows and the exchange rate. We now realize that it is important and that our persistent deficits are a symptom of a dearth of domestic savings. While the immediate priority of government is to stimulate spending to stave off recession, the longer-term need will be to boost savings for pensions, long-term care and the financing of mortgage deposits. There is a long period of austerity ahead.

The same is true of the public sector. In the immediate future it is a safe haven for employment and a necessary support for economic activity. In the longer term, structural deficits (negative savings) have to be reduced, which will bring severe constraints on public-spending growth and call into question expensive commitments such as generous public-sector pensions and the casual expansion of government bureaucracy and quangos.

The next illusion, the rebirth of British industry and enterprise, stems from a laudable willingness to embrace overseas partners and investors. The relaxed approach to the ownership of the car industry by Japanese and Indian firms, to electricity generation and distribution by French and German utility companies, and to Spanish banks makes Britain better placed in the long run to operate within a globalized world. But the price has been a shocking complacency about domestic capabilities. The paucity of British students coming through school and university with mathematical literacy, specialized sciences and modern languages means that there is an inadequate base for 'blue-skies' science, for applied science and engineering, and for global business negotiations. A generation's neglect of vocational skills has led to a situation where only Polish immigrants know how to repair leaking pipes and lay bricks. Such dependence is spreading up the occupational chain, unless future governments try to stop the rot within the school system. Instead of constant meddling, centralized intervention in every aspect of national life, the government has to focus on its core functions such as education and research.

Not least of the illusions is the belief that investment banking, mortgage-broking and complex financial product design were a source of national comparative advantage and wealth creation. The obsequious pilgrimage of Labour politicians to the City and their exaggerated deference to its concerns have led to a seriously unbalanced economy, more exposed to major financial shocks than others. I discussed in the penultimate chapter some of the reforms at national and international level needed to curb the destabilizing excesses of the financial sector. There may be a deeper problem. Thirty years ago, Britain had a 'Dutch disease', arising from the damaging effect on the exchange rate of oil and gas. What should have been an opportunity became a problem. The oil and gas reserves have now been run down (and, arguably, wasted), ending that disease. But it has been replaced by the 'Icelandic disease', whereby a banking sector outgrows its host economy, creating chronic financial instability. A brutal solution would be drastically to prune back the industry, as Mrs Thatcher did to coal-mining when Mr Scargill posed a threat to stability comparable to that created by Mr Adam Applegarth of Northern Rock, Sir Frank Godwin of RBS/Nat West and Mr Bob Diamond of Barclays today. But that would be destructive of much productive and genuinely wealth-creating activity in business services.

An alternative approach would be to anchor the currency and country in a bigger economic space, as Ireland has done in the eurozone. There is at present no great appetite for eurozone membership, and the eurozone has undoubted internal strains of its own. I have grown a little Eurosceptic in recent years and have recognized the short-term tactical merits of monetary and exchange rate independence. The current devaluation in particular could provide a helpful short-term stimulus to offset the recession. But when that independence looks to be largely illusory, with no enduring benefits, the attractions of external disciplines become much stronger. That conclusion is strengthened when we see that national fiscal disciplines have also proved illusory, and have allowed the accumulation of structural budget deficits which might have been subject to stronger peer group pressure in the eurozone. Should the eurozone navigate its way out of the current crisis quicker and with less damage than the UK, then the pressure in the UK for membership will grow strongly. Whether or not that particular option is open, there will have to be a radical economic rebalancing in which the financial services sector is relatively smaller and other traded activities, notably manufacturing, larger – and there is a parallel economic shift from the South East to the provinces.

The financial and economic crash has also exposed the weakening of social cohesion that has followed in the wake of Britain becoming an international financial centre. The amoral, cynical financial dealings which, we were assured, created wealth have contributed not just to instability but to a weakening of the wider 'social contract'. The tax system has been corrupted by the perceived need to defer to tax havens, the special needs of 'non-domiciled' residents, and the demand for capital gains to be treated more generously than earned income. There must now be a reconnection. We can surely learn from the open, social democratic Nordic economies and from Canada that a commitment to openness can be – and has to be – matched by a commitment at a national level to a balancing sense of 'fairness'. By this I do not mean a return to the illiberal, statist controls of the 1970s and before; the government is generally not very good at running complicated organizations and systems. But it should be possible, despite public spending constraints, through the generous but efficient provision of public goods, genuinely redistributive taxation and strong, solid safety nets for working families and pensioners, to remove extreme inequalities of wealth, income and opportunity; to recreate a sense that the country is a community; and to repair some of the damage that this great storm has wreaked. While there is crucial, urgent work to be done on the blocked financial plumbing and dangerous economic wiring, it is the job of the political class to redesign the home so that it is better able to withstand future disasters.

Bibliographic Note

This publication was written in some haste, against a background of rapidly changing and largely unprecedented events, without the prop and discipline of a comprehensive review of related literature. My main source has been the daily news and the commentary on it by business and economic journalists.

My approach has both the strengths and weaknesses of a commentary given by an active participant in the political debate, exposed to events and decision making at first hand, but also lacking detachment. Keynes once observed that 'all men of affairs are the slaves of some defunct economist'. I shall try, in my own case, to identify some of those defunct, as well as contemporary, sources of ideas.

———

In the **Introduction**, I try to locate the subject matter in the broad context of international economic, and specifically financial, integration: what we loosely call 'globalization'. I summarized the debates around globalization in a book I wrote a decade ago: *Glob-alization and Global Governance* (Royal Institute of International Affairs/Pinter, 1999). Two iconic texts around the subject of globalization are particularly relevant: Richard O'Brien's *Global Financial Integration: The End of Geography* (Royal Institute of International Affairs/Pinter, 1992), and Francis Fukuyama's *The End of History and the Last Man* (Hamish Hamilton, 1992). Since then, the most satisfactory and comprehensive analysis, and one that broadly reflects the author's view, has been in Martin Wolf's *Why Globalization Works* (Yale University Press, 2004), and also in Jagdish Bhagwati, *In Defence of Globalization* (Oxford University Press, 2007). There is an early, balanced assessment in P. Hirst and G. Thomson, *Globalization in Question* (Polity Press, 1996), and a comprehensive multidisciplinary survey in John Benyon and David Dunkerley, *Globalization: The Reader* (Athlone Press, 2000).

I also endeavour to locate the arguments in a historical context, and in particular the history of financial crashes and of economic cycles (which are often closely related). The classic texts on financial crises of which I have made good use are John Kenneth Galbraith's *A Short History of Financial Euphoria* (Penguin Books, 1990), Charles Kindleberger's *Manias, Panics and Crashes* (Basic Books, 1978), Hyman Minsky, *Stabilizing an Unstable Economy* (Yale University Press, 1986), and Edward Chancellor, *The Devil Take the Hindmost: A History of Financial Speculation* (Macmillan, 1999). There is a good contemporary study in John Calverley, *Bubbles and How to Survive Them* (Nicholas Brearley, 2004). Among academic studies that remind us that there have been many cyclical swings in commodity prices and economic growth are Phyllis Deane and W. A. Cole, *British Economic Growth 1688–1959* (Cambridge University Press, 1969), and Douglas North and R. P. Thomas, *The Rise of the Western World* (Cambridge University Press, 1973).

Of particular relevance to a cycle prominently featuring house prices are John Parry Lewis, *Building Cycles and Britain's Growth* (Macmillan, 1965), and Fred Harrison, *Boom Bust: House Prices, Banking and the Depression of 2010* (Shepherd Walwyn, 2008).

Periodic banking crises and economic cycles and the links between them were, I believe, first tackled systematically and theoretically by John Stuart Mill, 'Paper Currency and Commercial Distress', 1826, in *Collected Works of J. S. Mill*, ed. J. M. Robson, Vol. 4: *Essays on Economics and Society* (Routledge and Kegan Paul, 1967).

His insights were built upon by Alfred Marshall in *The Economics of Industry* (Macmillan, 1884). A good source on the history of economic thinking about cycles is W. W. Rostow, *Theorists of Economic Growth from David Hume to the Present* (Oxford University Press, 1990). Such theory as I understand on the subject I can trace back to my main undergraduate text: R. C. O. Matthews, *The Trade Cycle* (Cambridge University Press, 1959).

While there have been many boom and bust cycles in economic history, the one that matters and with which ominous parallels are now being drawn is that of the inter-war period. I returned to some familiar sources, notably John Kenneth Galbraith's *The Great Crash 1929* (Houghton Mifflin, 1988). Keynes's ideas are best surveyed in Robert Skidelsky's three-volume work, *John Maynard Keynes* (Macmillan, 1992–2001). The contrary, Austrian view of economics is to be found in the classic texts of von Mises, Bohm-Bauwerk, von Hayek and Schumpeter. These are briefly summarized in relation to economic cycles in Rostow (above). There is a restatement in a contemporary context in Sandy Chen's Equity Research paper for Panmure Gordon (23 September 2008).

In **Chapter 1** I take a worm's eye view of the crisis, seeing its emergence in Britain and in particular the first tangible sign of major trouble in the banking sector: the run on Northern Rock. This chapter depends more than most on contemporary reportage. But there is an exceptionally clear and balanced account in Alex Brummer's *The Crunch: The Scandal of Northern Rock and the Escalating Credit Crisis* (Random House Business Books, 2008). Alex Brummer is the *Daily Mail*'s City editor and he derives extra authority from his having warned about Northern Rock's business model as long ago as 2002. The House of Commons' Treasury Select Committee provided a very good and detailed account of Northern Rock, *The Run on the Rock*, Vol. 1 (Stationery Office, 2008). Another, more wide-ranging account is provided in Dan Atkinson and Larry Elliott's *Fantasy Island* (Constable, 2007), which deals with the dangerous overdependence of the UK on the pretensions and 'short-termism' of the City. An earlier, pre-crisis account in a similar vein is Will Hutton's *The State We're In* (Vintage, 1996). The role of the City in influencing economic policy under New Labour is discussed very well in Robert Peston's *Brown's Britain* (Short Books, 2008).

Chapter 2 draws upon contemporary press comment, but I made use of the historical material described above from Minsky, Kindleberger and Galbraith, as well as a World Bank study of more recent financial disasters: Gerard Caprio, *Episodes of Systemic and Borderline Financial Crisis* (World Bank, 2003). Perhaps the most perceptive and accurate analysis of the build-up to the current crisis is by Nouriel Roubini, of the New York Stern School of Business, who described the 'Twelve Steps to Disaster' on his blog <www.regemonitor.com>.

A key theme is the conduct of US monetary policy – and wider economic policy – in the years when Alan Greenspan was Chairman of the Federal Reserve. His own approach is set out in *The Age of Turbulence: Adventures in a New World* (Allen Lane, 2007). He is sympathetically reviewed in Bob Woodward, *Maestro: Greenspan's Fed and the American Boom* (Simon and Schuster, 2000), and with some hostility in Ravendra Batra, *Greenspan's Fraud: How Two Decades of Policies Have Undermined the Global Economy* (Palgrave Macmillan, 2005). Much of the statistical material is captured in the IMF's *Global Financial Stability Report: Containing Systemic Risks and Restoring Financial Soundness* (IMF, 2008).

For **Chapter 3**, the rich and varied history of the oil industry is captured best in Dan Yergin's book, *The Prize* (Simon and Schuster, 1991).

'Peak oil' theory is described in David Strachan, *The Last Oil*

Shock (John Murray, 2007), Kenneth Deffeyes, *Hubbert's Peak* (Princeton University Press, 2001), Jeremy Leggett, *Half Gone: Oil, Gas, Hot Air and the Global Energy Crisis* (Portobello, 2006), Matthew Simmonds, *Twilight in the Desert: The Coming Saudi Oil Shock and the World Economy* (John Wiley, 2005), Colin Campbell and Jean Lahererre, 'The End of Cheap Oil', *Scientific American*, March 1998. The counter-arguments are developed by Peter Odell, *Why Carbon Fuels Will Dominate the 21st Century's Global Energy Economy* (Multi-Science Publishing, 2004), and Morris Adelman, quoted in 'A Survey of Oil', *The Economist*, 30 April 2005.

The issues raised in **Chapter 4** go back to the controversies first raised by Thomas Malthus in *An Essay on the Principle of Population* (first edition, 1798), and later in Thomas Malthus, *Principles of Political Economy* (first edition, 1820). The circumstances surrounding the 2008 food price shock are described in the International Monetary Fund's *World Economic Outlook 2008*. There is a big literature on the distorted trade in foodstuffs, summarized in Kym Anderson and Will Martin, Introduction and Summary to *Agricultural Trade Reform and the Doha Development Agenda* (World Bank, 2005).

In **Chapter 5** the historical context relies heavily on Angus Maddison's *Monitoring the World Economy 1820–1992* (OECD Development Centre, 1995). Maddison also explains the necessity and methodology for using purchasing power parity-based measurements of GDP when comparing countries at different levels of development over long periods of time. Other major pieces of historical scholarship are Dwight Perkins, *Agricultural Development in China, 1368–1968* (Aldine, 1969), and D. Kumar and M. Desai, *Cambridge Economic History of India* (Cambridge University Press, 1983).

The significance of the economic rise of China is now described in countless publications. One of the earliest was Nicholas Lardy, *China and the World Economy* (Institute for International Economics, 1994). More recent are Will Hutton, *The Writing on the Wall: China and the West in the 21st Century* (Little Brown, 2007), and James Kynge, *China Shakes the World: The Rise of a Hungry Nation* (Orion, 2006). The monetary linkages that connect China to the asset bubbles in Western economies are best described in Graham Turner, *The Credit Crunch* (Pluto Press, 2008). The first comprehensive account of how Chinese growth might help to create a world with low or no inflation is in Roger Bootle, *The Death of Inflation* (Nicholas Brearley, 1996). My own paper, *China and India: The New Giants* (Royal Institute of International Affairs, 1996), describes the relative performance and potential of the two emerging economies.

The impact of Chinese manufacturing on wage levels and income distribution in Western countries is discussed in Raphael Kaplinsky's *Globalization, Poverty and Inequality* (Polity Press, 2005), Adrian Wood's *North–South Trade: Employment and Inequality* (Oxford University Press, 1994), and Ravendra Batra's *The Myth of Free Trade: The Pooring of America* (Scribner's, 1993). A counterview is in M. Slaughter and P. Swagel, *The Effect of Globalization on Wages in Advanced Economies*, IMF Working Papers (IMF, 1997), and P. Krugman and R. Lawrence, *Trade, Jobs and Wages*, NBER Working Paper 34478 (National Bureau of Economic Research, 1993). The history of the protectionist responses to low wage competition is described in a book I wrote a quarter of a century ago: V. Cable, *Protectionism and Industrial Decline* (Hodder and Stoughton, 1983), and drew specifically on Ephraim Lipson, *The Economic History of England*, Vol 2: *The Age of Mercantilism*, 6th ed. (A&C Black, 1956). The general arguments are discussed very effectively in Deepak Lal, *The Resurrection of the Pauper Labour Argument*, Thames Essay No. 28 (Trade Policy Research Centre, 1981).

Chapter 6 deals more widely with the political reactions to globalization and alternative models. There is a good statement of the 'green' rejection of 'free trade' and economic interpretation in Tim Lang and Colin Hiness' book *The New Protectionism* (Earthscan Publications, 1993), and, later, in George Monbiot's publications, including 'Protectionism makes you rich', *Guardian*, 9 September 2008. Coming from a different, socially conservative direction, but reaching similar conclusions, is John Gray, *Beyond the New Right* (Routledge, 1993), and B. Jones's 'Globalization versus Community', *New Political Economy*, Vol. 2, No. 1 (1997). Hostility to globalization from a more traditional 'leftist' standpoint comes, *inter alia*, from Noam Chomsky, who, like Lenin, sees the process as an expression of imperialism, as in *9-11* (Seven Stories Press, 2001), or in Harry Shutt, *The Trouble with Capitalism: An Enquiry into the Causes of Global Economic Failure* (Zed Books, 1998). Bob Rowthorn questioned the merits of liberal immigration from the standpoint of the working class in developed countries in *Prospect* magazine in August 2006. A distinctive analysis is contained in David Singh Grewal, *Network Power: The Social Dynamics of Globalization* (Yale University Press, 2008). The distributional aspects of an open, liberal system are discussed in a helpful way in William Bernstein, *Splendid Exchange: How Trade Shaped the World* (Atlantic Books, 2008).

There is a discussion of the 'politics of identity' and how it might re-emerge in the wake of the Cold War in my two Demos pamphlets: *The World's New Fissures: Identities in Crisis* (1994), and *Multiple Identity: Living with the New Politics of Identity* (2005). The attempts of the political right to develop what I call 'modernized xenophobia' are best captured in Giulio Tremonti's *The Fear and the Hope* (2008) (I have relied on English commentaries on a book published in Italian), and James Goldsmith's *Le Piège* (*The Trap*) (Macmillan, 1996). The nearest the USA has come to producing a figure on the right articulating a similar economic message is Pat Buchanan, *Where the Right Went Wrong* (Thomas Dunne Books, 2004).

The notion that national (or broader) identities might spill over into conflicts about the international order are described in particularly apocalyptic terms in Samuel P. Huntington's *The Clash of Civilizations* (Simon and Schuster, 1997), and more subtly in Michel Albert, *Capitalism versus Capitalism* (Whurr, 1995). Concern that such competition might result in an exclusive, discriminatory form of regional integration are expressed by Jagdish Bhagwati, *Termites in the Trading System: How Preferential Agreements Undermine Free Trade* (Council for Foreign Relations, 2008), and in Vincent Cable and David Henderson, *Trade Blocs: The Future of Regional Integration* (Royal Institute of International Affairs, 1994). The uses and abuses of the concept of 'economic security' are discussed in my *International Affairs* article 'What is Economic Security?' (April 1995).

The debate around what kind of capitalism should emerge from the experiences of the recent past has been touched on in the debate on Greenspan's legacy (see notes to Chapter 2). Those who consistently argued for a less permissive approach to financial markets include Joseph Stiglitz, *The Roaring Nineties: Why We're Paying the Price for the Greediest Decade in History* (Allen Lane, 2003), and George Soros, *The New Paradigm for Financial Markets* (Public Affairs, 2008). The case against Greenspan's fatalistic approach to the regulation of financial markets is best described in a series of exchanges in the *Financial Times*: Martin Wolf, 'Why financial regulation is both difficult and essential' (15 April 2008); Henry Kaufmann, 'The principles of sound regulation' (5 August 2008); also his *On Money and Markets: A Wall Street Memoir* (McGraw-Hill, 2000).

Chapter 7 refers to the extremes of inequality. There is often a confusing (sometimes deliberately confusing) distinction between stock of assets (wealth) and flow of income. The main contemporary sources on global wealth and income are helpfully pulled together in Stephen Haseler's *Meltdown: How the Masters* *of the Universe Destroyed the West's Power and Prosperity* (Forum Press, 2008).

Underlying the policy debate in Chapter 7 about what can and should now sensibly be done is a theoretical argument. Until the current crisis, there was a wide belief in the academic world that financial markets were best explained by the 'efficient market hypothesis' – part of a broader neoclassical approach that assumes rational behaviour by companies and consumers. Markets do not, on this view, 'misbehave', but correctly factor in all the available information. It follows that asset prices are always 'correct' and do not manifest themselves as 'bubbles'. There are many recent sources explaining why this approach has proved to be dangerously wrong, among them George Cooper's *The Origin of Financial Crises* (Harriman House, 2008), John Calverley's *Bubbles and How to Survive Them* (Nicholas Brearley, 2004), and also George Soros (see p. 164). The definitive explanation of why markets do not work when there is a collapse of trust is provided in George Akerlof, 'The Market for Lemons: Quality, Uncertainty and the Market Mechanism', *Quarterly Journal of Economics*, 84 (3) (1970), 488–500.

The arguments for aggressive monetary policy in the face of a severe credit contraction are dealt with in the classic monetarist text: Milton Friedman and Anna Schwarz, *A Monetary History of the United States 1867–1960* (Princeton University Press, 1963). The various policy initiatives to improve monetary policy – taking account of asset markets – are discussed in detail in my 2008 annual lecture to the Institute of Fiscal Studies, and are set out in C. Goodhart and A. Persaud, 'A proposal for how to avoid the next crash', *Financial Times*, 31 January 2008, who describe countercyclical adequacy rules; see also *Making Macroprudential Concerns Operational* (IMF, 2004). The idea that measures of inflation should include asset prices was originally mooted in Irving Fisher, *The Purchasing Power of Money* (Macmillan, 1911), and has been updated as in Sushil Wadhwani, 'Should Monetary Policy Respond to Asset Price Bubbles? Revisiting the Debate', *National Institute Economic Review*, 206 (1) (2008), 25–34.

A good discussion on how to reform bonuses is in R. Rajan, 'Bankers' pay is deeply flawed', *Financial Times*, 9 January 2008. The broader question of how to reconcile the necessity for maintaining a commitment to an open, globalized economy with a sense of fairness and equity is addressed in, *inter alia*, Joseph Stiglitz, *Making Globalization Work* (W. W. Norton, 2006).

Acknowledgements

This book was written in some haste in the gaps left in a very busy few months in the summer and autumn of 2008, as the storm was raging. Because of the speed involved I have been unable to rely on the comments and advice of colleagues and friends to the extent that I normally do, and any errors of fact and interpretation are mine alone.

I have benefited in terms of ideas from the community of British financial and economic journalists and columnists who provided regular, understandable commentary on the crisis. Several, like Alex Brummer, Martin Wolf, Larry Elliott, Will Hutton, Gillian Tett, Roger Bootle and Anatole Kaletsky, have published their own analyses separately, in varying degrees of detail, on particular aspects of the crisis.

I also want to acknowledge the role of my political colleagues who have been generous with their time, helping me to understand the issues and their political significance, including Matthew Oakeshott, Chris Huhne and our party leader, Nick Clegg. And I still owe a lot to my former colleagues at Shell who taught me about 'think the unthinkable' and 'the art of the long view'.

I am grateful to my PA, Joan Bennett, and my Westminster staff, Sally Duncan and Paul Scaping, for typing parts of the manuscript in their spare time. My biggest debt is to my wife, Rachel, who typed most of the manuscript, as well as providing constant encouragement and, on her farm, a haven of peace in which to write.

Finally, I am grateful too to my literary agent, Georgina Capel, of Capel and Land, for encouragement to write – and complete – the book, and to the extremely professional publishing team at Atlantic Books.

Index